HANDY
PET CARE
GUIDES

Choosing &
Looking After Your

Cat

This is a **FLAME TREE** book
First published in 2014

Publisher and Creative Director: Nick Wells
Senior Project Editor: Catherine Taylor
Picture Research: Victoria Lyle, Gemma Walters
Art Director: Mike Spender
Layout Design: Jane Ashley
Illustrator: Ann Biggs
Copy Editor: Colette Campbell
Indexer: Eileen Cox

Special thanks to: Esme Chapman and Emma Chafer

FLAME TREE PUBLISHING
Crabtree Hall, Crabtree Lane
Fulham, London SW6 6TY
United Kingdom

www.flametreepublishing.com

First published 2014

14 16 18 17 15
1 3 5 7 9 10 8 6 4 2

© 2014 Flame Tree Publishing Ltd

A CIP record for this book is available from the British Library upon request.

ISBN 978-1-78361-229-1

Printed in Singapore

Picture Credits:
Ardea: John Daniels 202, 227; Jean Michel Labat 221. **Corbis:** 84 all, 138; Christie's Images 27; Don Mason 129; Fine Art Photographic Library 26; Hulton-Deutsch Collection 209; Krista Kennell/ZUMA 37; Mediscan 194; Pat Doyle 36; Philip Gould 173; Robert Holmes 23; Roger Wood 20; SGO/Image Point FR 208. **DK Images:** 3 br, 45, 48ml, 48tr, 48br, 48tl, 48ct, 48tm, 48bm, 49bl, 49br, 49mr, 49tl, 49ml, 49c, 49lb, 49bm, 49tm, 65, 77, 82, 89, 99, 112, 119, 120, 122, 140, 164, 165, 169, 177, 178, 193, 200, 207, 213, 241. **FLPA:** Mitsuaki Iwago 86; Angela Hampton 28–29, 149, 157; Armin Floreth 80; David T Grewcock 92; Gerard Lacz 32; Giesbert Kühne 5 br, 151; Konrad Wothe 153; Malcolm Schuyl 19; Martin B Withers 212; Mike Lane 134; Panda Photo 48 bl, 150; Terry Whittaker 17. **Foundry Arts:** 31, 31, 33, 35, 41, 53, 59, 182. **Mary Evans Picture Library:** 25. **Marc Henrie:** 8–9, 10, 12, 13, 14, 15, 38, 40, 55, 64, 67, 68, 71, 72, 76, 78, 79, 87, 88, 91, 93, 95, 96, 103, 104, 106, 107, 108, 109, 110, 113, 114, 115, 118, 124, 127, 128, 135, 136, 137, 146, 148, 155, 158, 161, 162, 163, 166, 170, 171, 175, 179, 180, 183, 184, 189, 190bl, 191, 198, 203, 206, 223, 226, 229, 235, 236. **RSPCA Photolibrary:** 196, 211; Geoff du Feu 190tl; Angela Hampton 197, 205, 215, 217, 218, 231, 232, 233; Des Cartwright 230; Nick Withey 228. **Shutterstock:** 69, 139; aceshot1 132; Africa Studio 195; Anna Dzondzua 42; Alexey Demidov 126, 201; Ariusz Nawrocki 133; Ben Heys 131; Byelikova Oksana 185; Cherry-Merry 75; Denis Tabler 225; Dusan Zidar 100–116; Ekaterina Cherkashina 48 cb, 48mr; Eric Isselée 52; Erik Lam 49 tr; Ermolaev Alexander 121; fotorro 156; Galina Barskaya 145; Gleb Semenjuk 167; Graham S Klotz 7; H Tuller 1br, 57; Igor Stepovik 97; Ilyas Kalimullin 63; J Helgason 73; J Kitan 90; Jakub Zak 125; Joy Brown 199; Leach 61; Lois M Kosch 147; Lubava 5 tr, 34, 105; Mary Bingham 60; Mauro Matacchione 4 bl, 123; mdmmikle 70; Melissa Ann Kilhenny 74; Michelle D Milliman 3 c; Miroslav Hlavko 85; Misha Shiyanov 11; Monkey Business Images 181; Nat Ulrich 56, 159; Niek Goossen 219; Paisit Teeraphatsakool 142–143; Perrush 130; Polina Lobanova 176; Robert Redelowski 237; Schubbel 141; s-dmit 54; Sharon Meredith 117; Shawn Hine 81; Simone van den Berg 1 c, 4tl, 43; Tatiana Morozova 62; Tony Campbell 58, 152; Utekhina Anna 44; Vladimir Melnik 111; WilleeCole 83; Zhorov Igor Vladimirovich 187. **TopFoto:** ARPL/HIP 21.

HANDY
PET CARE
GUIDES

Choosing &
Looking After Your

Cat

LEE HARPER

**FLAME TREE
PUBLISHING**

Contents

Introduction

There is nothing more comforting after a stressful day than curling up on the sofa with your favourite feline friend. Cats are more than just cute pets; they offer intelligent company thanks to their individual personalities. Popular throughout history and proven relievers of stress, cats are self-sufficient and impart a sense of relaxation. In this guide, discover comprehensive information detailing everything you need to know to care for your cat successfully.

With practical information on the dangers faced by both indoor and outdoor cats, travelling with your kitty and dealing with feline ailments, *Choosing & Looking After Your Cat* is a great resource for owners who have their cat's best interests at heart. Ideal for those considering getting their first kitten as well as the more experienced cat owner, the book contains useful information on how to prepare for the arrival of a new cat, how to provide the best nutrition and what to do in a medical emergency. Key aspects of pet cat ownership are covered, from taking care of and training kittens to details on how to accommodate an older cat.

Detailed diagrams and in-depth descriptions of the anatomy, senses and the appearance of the cat will allow the reader to know their animal from head to paw. Feline instinct and behaviour will be brought to life as the book guides you through the many, varying aspects of a cat's psychological make-up including hunting and communication.

Choosing & Looking After Your Cat is an indispensable guide for all cat lovers – from first time owners to those who are certified cat people – there is something for everyone.

For the Love of
Cats

Cats in Human History

God made the cat in order to give man the pleasure of caressing the tiger' (author unknown). From ancient times, humans and cats have shared a unique relationship. Of all the domesticated animals, it is cat that seems closest to its wild roots – and therein lies its mystique. Despite the dog's reputation as man's best friend, it is the cat that is the most popular pet in homes throughout most of the world.

A Growing Population

There is an estimated 600 million house cats worldwide. With a human population of roughly 6.6 billion, that means there is one cat for almost every ten people on the planet. Moreover, the popularity of the feline continues to grow.

A 2007 survey by the American Pet Products Association found the country with the most cats is the USA with

◄ Owning a cat can be therapeutic and an antidote to the stresses of fast-paced modern life.

88.3 million felines; almost 15 million more cats than dogs. China rates second with about 55 million felines.
In the United Kingdom, approximately one out of every four households has a family cat. In the US; more than
a third of households have a feline. Ninety-two per cent of pet cats are mixed breed or 'moggies'.

What makes the cat so popular?

More than 50 per cent of people surveyed say they keep a pet for love and companionship. The fast pace of
life, increased stresses and demanding work life of the modern world often means individuals lack the time
or energy to develop close relationships. A pet can help fill that gap and be both rewarding and therapeutic.

Cats make ideal pets. They are less demanding than a dog, are clean, fastidious, and relatively quiet.
A cat is content to live an indoor existence making it suitable for anyone who lives in a high-rise flat. Beyond
convenience, the cat has a definite mystique – loving yet independent, elegant yet playful, cautious yet
bold, mysterious yet familiar.

Working Cats

Most house cats enjoy a privileged lifestyle; the feline
equivalent of royalty with servants providing all their
comforts. Yet, some cats work for their living, for the cat
is the world's most accomplished rat catcher – a job
respected since earliest recorded history. In ancient times,

◀ Many farms keep working cats as a way of controlling the rats
and mice.

the cat was recognized and valued for its ability to keep the granaries of the world free of rats and mice. Some historians theorize that the Egyptians held the domestic cat in such high esteem due to this special feline talent.

Not all mouse-catching felines have worked in an agricultural setting. Accounts from Exeter Cathedral from 1305 through 1467 include a salary for a succession of cats. The wage was to supplement the diet of the official cat, who was expected to control the pest population of the cathedral.

In 1883, a cat named Peter also received a wage to rid the British Home Office of rodents. The tradition of employing a black cat for vermin control in the Home Office continued for almost a century.

Feral Cats

Not all cats maintain a close relationship with humankind. Wild or 'feral' cats are the descendants of domesticated felines that have strayed or been abandoned. Once homeless, feral cats live and breed according to their own resources. Although the mother cat may once have been a family pet, when she gives birth in the wild, her offspring are never socialized with humans. The kittens are feral. While some ferals live a solitary existence, they are more commonly found in large groups called feral colonies. The largest feral cat population in the world is in Rome, Italy, where between 250,000–350,000 feral cats live, organized into about 2,000 colonies and residing in such famous landmarks as the Coliseum and Vatican City.

The Rise of the Domestic Cat

More than any other domesticated animal, the cat has endured wild swings of fortune in its relationship with man. At one time revered as a god, the cat has also been reviled as a devil. Yet, no matter its status, the cat has always fascinated humankind. Whether living in the baking hot desert or frozen fjord, from mud hut to exotic palace, from ancient tombs to the modern urban jungle, the domestic cat has endured and thrived through the ages.

Descended from the Wildcats

Fifty million years ago, during the Eocene period, a weasel-like creature called miacids hunted in the forests. From this fierce creature the meat-eating carnivores evolved. The biological order, carnivora, is divided into several families including Felidae, the family of large and small cats. The family Felidae is divided into six genus including Felis, which includes the smaller felines such as the bobcat, ocelot, serval and the domestic cat.

There has been much debate over the evolutionary relationship of the small wildcats and the modern domestic cat (*Felis silvestris catus*). DNA evidence published in 2007 concluded that domestic cats are

▶ Our domestic cats belong to the same genus as the smaller wildcats, such as this tree-dwelling Margay.

descended from at least five founding females of the African (also known as the 'North African' or 'Sardinian') wildcat (*Felis silvestris lybica*). As the first cats accompanied man in his travels, there was probably subsequent interbreeding between the domestic cat and other subspecies of wildcats including the European wildcat (*F.s. silvestris*), the Central Asian wildcat (*F.s. ornata*), the sub-Saharan African wildcat (*F.s. cafra*) and the Chinese desert cat (*F.s. bieti*).

In from the Wild

It is difficult to pinpoint exactly when cats were first domesticated. Ancestors resembling modern cats first appeared about ten million years ago, but they were completely wild and did not associate with humans. The record of the cohabitation of cats and humans is buried in the mists of time. Ancient man was a nomadic hunter. As civilization progressed, humans lived a more settled lifestyle and learned to farm, raising grain crops such as wheat and barley. Stockpiling a portion of the harvest each winter, the grain attracted rats, mice and birds, and these, in turn, attracted wildcats. Gradually, the wildcats and humans formed a mutually beneficial relationship. It is easy to imagine the cats becoming progressively tamer and eventually fully domesticated.

The oldest archaeological evidence of a domesticated cat was found in the ancient Neolithic village of Shillourokambos on the Greek island of Cyprus. There are no wild cats native to Cyprus, yet the remains of a small cat were discovered buried just 40 centimetres from a 9,500-year-old human grave, suggesting that the cat may have been brought to the island as a treasured pet and buried with its master.

The next evidence of domestication was found in Haçilar, Turkey where images of female figurines dated around sixth century BC were discovered carrying catlike figures in their arms.

▶ Recent scientific research has shown that the African wildcat is a direct ancestor of the domestic cat.

The Golden Age of the Cat

The first wall painting of a cat wearing a collar, a sure sign of domestication, appears on a fifth dynasty Egyptian tomb in Saqqara (Old Kingdom, circa 2500–2350 BC). By the twelfth dynasty (Middle Kingdom, circa 1976–1793 BC), small cats with ticked coats were frequent subjects in Egyptian art. By the twenty-second dynasty, the golden age of the Pharaohs, King Osorkon ritually endowed a white cat with supreme power in a temple ceremony. Cats became divine.

So valued were the cats, even King Ptolemy Aultete, father of Cleopatra, was unable to save a Roman who had accidentally killed a cat. The man was hanged. The Persian king, Cambyse II, won the battle of Peluse by commanding his soldiers strap cats to their shields. The Egyptians surrendered rather than injure the felines.

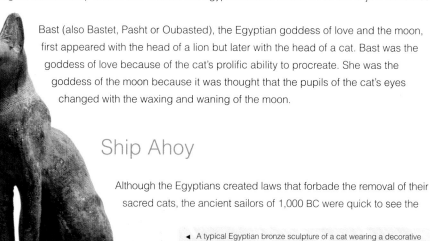

Bast (also Bastet, Pasht or Oubasted), the Egyptian goddess of love and the moon, first appeared with the head of a lion but later with the head of a cat. Bast was the goddess of love because of the cat's prolific ability to procreate. She was the goddess of the moon because it was thought that the pupils of the cat's eyes changed with the waxing and waning of the moon.

Ship Ahoy

Although the Egyptians created laws that forbade the removal of their sacred cats, the ancient sailors of 1,000 BC were quick to see the

◄ A typical Egyptian bronze sculpture of a cat wearing a decorative collar, dating from *C.* 600 BC.

► The Egyptians valued cats for their hunting abilities, as suggested by this painting from *C.* 1400–1425 BC.

advantage of having cats aboard ship during long voyages to protect their food supplies from damage by rodents, so Phoenician and Greek sailors smuggled cats out of Egypt.

The cats brought aboard the trading vessels may have 'jumped ship' at various ports and in this manner cats spread through Asia and Europe. Archaeological evidence indicates that the Romans were the first to bring cats to the British Isles. As the powerful seafaring nations crossed the Atlantic Ocean in the 1600s, they in turn introduced the domestic cat to the new world.

The Far East and the Orient

Cats reached China around 400 AD. The silk growers of China appreciated the cat's hunting abilities so employed them to prevent rats and mice from destroying silkworm cocoons at a time when silk trading was vital to the economy. By the twelfth century AD the yellow and white 'lion-cats' were particularly valued as pets.

Cats were introduced in Japan around the sixth century. According to custom, every temple owned two cats in order to keep mice away from the manuscripts. In the Middle Ages, the Japanese distinguished good luck cats by their tortoiseshell fur and malevolent cats by their forked tail and their ability to change themselves into witches. Disciples of yoga felt the sleeping position of the cat was the ideal position to regulate vital body fluids. A symbol of purity, cats became the bridge between Buddha and his faithful followers. The Kyoto palace opened its doors to a white cat that had given birth to five kittens. A temple was dedicated to the cat named Maneki Neko, called the beckoning cat, seated with one paw raised in greeting.

In the twelfth century, Sultan El-Daher-Beybars bequeathed a park for stray cats called Gheytel-Qouttah or The Cat Orchards; its feral cats were fed for many years. The Arabs of the seventh century believed cats had

▶ In Japan, these ceramic cats with one paw raised are placed in front of a home to ensure good fortune.

a pure spirit, unlike the unclean spirit of dogs. According to legend, when Mohammed's cat, Muezza, was sleeping in the prophet's sleeve, the prophet chose to cut the garment rather than disturb his companion.

Indian epics Ramayana and Mahabharata, 500 BC, also refer to pet cats. Indians worshipped a feline goddess of maternity, Sasti, the protector of children. There was a time when Hindus were obligated to feed at least one cat. The Siamese cat of Siam (Thailand) could only be owned by royalty and was bestowed as a gift to visiting dignitaries.

Reviled in Europe of the Middle Ages

And so the domesticated cat spread throughout the world, admired for its hunting ability, fertility and beauty … until the Middle Ages. Because cats were associated with femininity, sensuality and sexuality, the Church of the Middle Ages attributed evil powers to felines, and set out to destroy the myths and pagan worship associated with the cat. Cats became symbols of evil and Satan. Hundreds of thousands of cats were crucified, tortured, skinned alive or thrown into the fire as companions of witches. Once a demigod, the cat's fall from grace lasted almost two centuries.

The Plague

As the feline population dwindled, the rodent population thrived. By 1799, bubonic plague, the Black Death, spread rampant through Europe, transmitted by the fleas on grey sewer rats. The cat's skill as a hunter of vermin was desperately needed. Its reputation was salvaged. Owning a cat was back in fashion. The Royal Navy even decreed that every ship must carry two cats on board in order to ward off rodents.

▶ The spread of the plague via rats helped to restore the reputation of the cat as a valuable companion.

The Return to Favour

While the cat was once more acceptable, it was not viewed as a pet in the same way as a dog. Then in the late 1800s, Louis Pasteur's theories regarding microscopic microbes led to people developing a phobia about animals carrying germs. With their reputation for cleanliness, cats were exempt from the fears of contamination. Thus began another period of feline popularity. Writers, philosophers and artists, became inspired by the feline form and personality.

The Modern Age

As the popularity of cats grew, and their beauty recognized, it was inevitable that fanciers would want to compare their cats with those of others. The first contemporary cat show was held in 1871 in England and was organized by Harrison Weir, considered the father of the cat fancy. Enthusiasts began selective breeding of the domesticated cat, establishing pedigree records, developing new breeds and breeding to type. The number of cat breeds grew from a mere 20 in 1960, to over 70 breeds recognized by various cat registries around the world by the end of the twentieth century. New hybrid breeds continue to be developed to the current day.

◄ George Sheridan Knowles' *Kittens* (c. 1890–1930) shows how cats had once again become acceptable as pets.

► In the nineteenth century cats became a popular subject for paintings, such as this one by Julius Adam.

How
Cats
work

Anatomy, Physiology and Appearance

While effortlessly fitting into our modern environment, the domestic cat's unique physical appearance and mental abilities are the hereditary gifts of its historical role as a nocturnal hunter. Like its wild cousins, the family cat possesses retractable claws, remarkable night vision, a keen sense of hearing, and a highly flexible, muscular body. The cat's physical attributes are complemented by its active intelligence, excellent memory, keen analytical skills, and an aptitude for learning from experience … and of course its fabled inexhaustible curiosity.

Skeleton and Physique

The Skeleton

The feline physique is designed for powerful and fluid movements needed to stalk and capture wild prey. The cat skeleton is composed of 230 bones compared to the human's 206. Allowing for a variation in tail length dependent upon the breed of cat, almost 10 per cent of a cat's bones are in the tail. The cat has 30 vertebrae in its backbone, five more than a human's. The extra bones allow for the backbone's flexibility that contributes to the cat's athletic prowess. The cat's clavicle bones are free-floating which is why its body can fit through any opening its head can pass through.

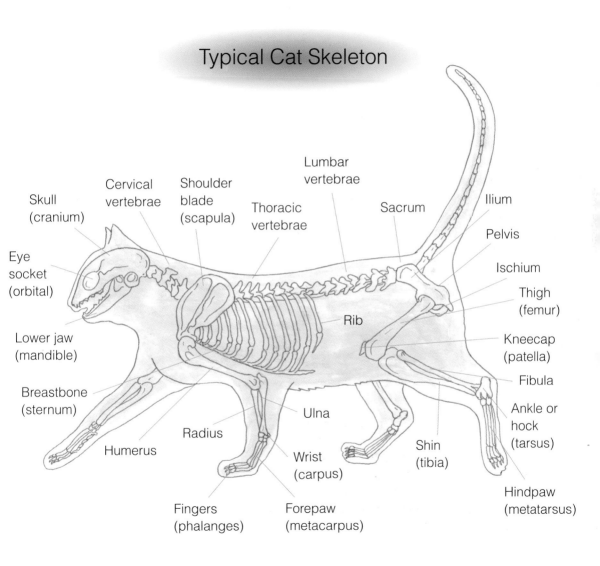

Typical Cat Skeleton

Skull (cranium)

Cervical vertebrae

Shoulder blade (scapula)

Thoracic vertebrae

Lumbar vertebrae

Sacrum

Ilium

Pelvis

Ischium

Thigh (femur)

Eye socket (orbital)

Lower jaw (mandible)

Rib

Kneecap (patella)

Fibula

Breastbone (sternum)

Ulna

Ankle or hock (tarsus)

Radius

Wrist (carpus)

Shin (tibia)

Humerus

Fingers (phalanges)

Forepaw (metacarpus)

Hindpaw (metatarsus)

The overall skeleton provides a framework for the body. The ribs and sternum (breastbone) protect the heart and lungs from injury while the skull protects the brain and eyes. There are specialized bones in the ear that allow the cat to hear.

The cat skeleton is composed of four types of bones: long, short, irregular and flat. The long bones of the legs are elongated cylinders with hollow shafts that contain the marrow that manufactures red blood corpuscles. Short bones, including the toes and kneecaps, have a spongy core surrounded by compact bone. The vertebrae of the spine are irregular bones, similar in composition to short bones except for the unusual shape. Flat bones consist of a thin central layer of spongy bone sandwiched between two layers of compact bone and form the skull, the shoulder blades, and the pelvis.

Bones are living organs composed of calcium and phosphorus, with their own blood supply and nerves. The long bones of the legs grow from immature bone located near the ends called the epiphyseal or growth plates. Once growth is complete, usually around a year of age, the growth plates 'close', becoming hardened with calcium and minerals, a process called mineralization. Until the growth plates harden, they are particularly vulnerable to injury. Epiphyseal fractures are common in kittens near the wrist (carpus) and the knee (stifle).

The Muscular System

The cat has 500 skeletal muscles. There are two basic types of muscles: smooth and striated. The smooth muscles are involuntary – the individual has no control

◄ The long bones of a cat's legs are usually fully formed after around a year of growth.

Muscular System

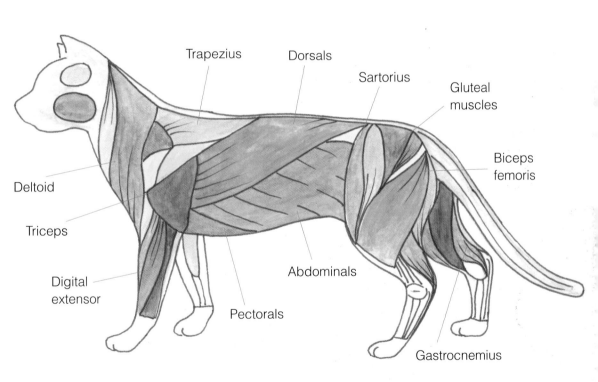

Trapezius

Dorsals

Sartorius

Gluteal
muscles

Deltoid

Biceps
femoris

Triceps

Digital
extensor

Abdominals

Pectorals

Gastrocnemius

over their function. They are the muscles associated with the internal organs such as the intestines, stomach and bladder. Striated muscles are predominately attached to bones of the skeleton and are under the conscious control of the individual. The striated muscles are what allow the cat to walk, eat, to move its eyes, ears and tail.

Development of the muscles reflects the physical needs and abilities of the cat. The hindquarters of the cat are thickly muscled so the hind legs can provide the explosive power needed to leap and pounce on prey when hunting. The strong muscles of the cat's lower bottom jaw enable it to grasp and hold its prey securely.

Claws

Like its skeleton and musculature, the cats' specialized claws and dentition evolved from its hunting past. The cat has five toes and claws on each front foot and four on each back foot. The fifth claw on the front foot is located higher on the inside of the leg and is called the dewclaw. The dewclaw acts like a thumb, aiding the cat to grip when attacking prey or climbing. Cats become stuck up in trees because their claws are constructed perfectly for climbing up, but curve the wrong way for climbing down.

The claws are made of keratin, the same protein that forms the outer layer of the skin and human nails.

Claw Retraction and Extension

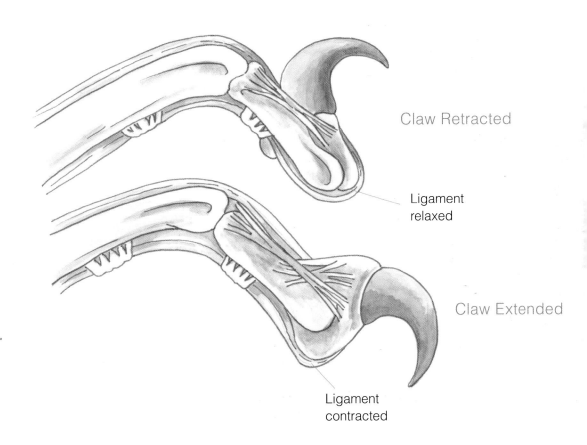

Claw Retracted

Ligament
relaxed

Claw Extended

Ligament
contracted

A blood vessel called the 'quick' runs through the centre of the nail. The quick does not reach to the end of the actual point of the claw allowing you to trim the nail. If you cut into them the nail will bleed.

What makes the cat unique in the carnivore family is that its claws retract, allowing the cat is to silently stalk its prey. As the cat attacks, specialized ligaments contract and the claws flash out to grip the prey. Because the claws retract when not needed, they stay very sharp.

The Polydactyl

While most cats have a total of 18 toes and claws, some cats are more generously endowed. Polydactyl is the name used to describe cats with extra toes and claws – sometimes up to seven on each foot.

Also known as hyperdactyl or supernumerary digits, extra toes is not a rare trait in felines. The innermost extra toes on the front paws are often opposable, allowing some cats to use their front paws like hands in an almost human-like manner. While polydactylism can be hereditary or a spontaneous mutation, it is a condition and not a breed of cat. The most famous colony of polydactyl cats was owned by American writer, Ernest Hemingway. The multi-toed descendents of Hemingway's original cats still live in his former home in Key West, Florida where they are protected by law.

▶ Extra toes are not uncommon in cats; this polydactyl kitten has six digits on each of her front paws.

The Teeth

Feline dentition is designed for tearing and biting, not chewing. In the wild, the cat tears a piece from the carcass and swallows it whole. Teeth come in four types. Incisors are small front teeth, closely spaced, ideal for ripping and scraping flesh off bone. The canines are the pointed fangs or eyeteeth made for holding prey down, killing and ripping. Because cats don't chew in the classic sense, the premolars and molars slice food into chunks small enough to swallow. The premolar and first molar function to shear meat like a pair of scissors. The cat's teeth are symmetrical on each side of the jaw, but differ in number from the top jaw to the lower jaw. The upper jaw contains six incisors, two canines, six premolars and two molars. The lower jaw contains six incisors, two canines, only four premolars and two molars.

Like a human baby, a kitten is born without teeth. The deciduous or 'milk teeth' begin to appear at about four weeks of age. By six weeks of age, 26 deciduous teeth are present: 12 incisors, four canines and ten premolars (no molars). Between 13 to 30 weeks of age, kittens lose their baby teeth and the permanent adult teeth come in. By six months old, the kitten has 30 permanent teeth. By comparison, a dog has 42 permanent teeth.

◄ A cat's powerful canine teeth are designed to capture, hold down and kill prey, and to rip flesh.

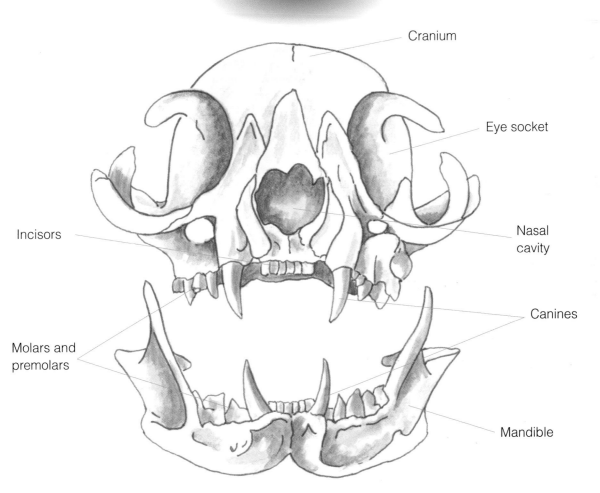

Cat Skull

Cranium

Eye socket

Incisors

Nasal cavity

Canines

Molars and premolars

Mandible

Skin and Coat

The Skin

Cats have particularly loose-fitting skin that allows them to defend themselves by wiggling around in the grip of a predator. The veterinarian also finds this convenient when giving an injection or fluids under the skin. The scruff is the loose skin at the back of the neck. The mother cat grips her kittens by the scruff to carry them. Even as an adult, most cats tend to become quiet and passive when gripped by the skin on the back of the neck; hence the expression 'scruffing' the cat. This behaviour can be useful to subdue an injured or uncooperative cat. Never attempt to carry an adult cat by the scruff, as it is too heavy and should be supported under the rump and chest. The tough outer layer of the skin is called the epidermis. As the outer cells erode, cells underneath mature and move up to replace them. The thickness of the epidermis varies. The more exposed areas, such as the head and back, are thicker than less exposed areas such as the armpits and belly.

The deeper layer of the skin, called the dermis, contains hair follicles, blood vessels, nerves and sebaceous oil glands. Cats do not sweat through their skin but through their paw pads and nose. They lose water by panting rather than sweating. Hair follicles and sebaceous glands are more numerous on the back than on the belly.

◄ A cat's loose-fitting skin enables it to be carried safely when young, as well as escape predators.

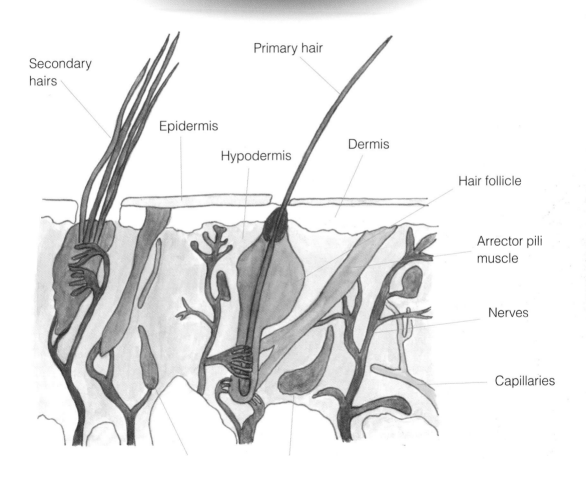

Cross Section of Cat's Skin

Secondary hairs

Primary hair

Epidermis

Hypodermis

Dermis

Hair follicle

Arrector pili muscle

Nerves

Capillaries

The Coat

Like claws, hair is composed of keratin. Each follicle can grow a single hair. A kitten is born with all the follicles it will ever possess. Most cats have four basic types of hair: guard, awn, down hair and vibrissae. The average adult has about 1,000 down hairs for every 300 awn hairs and 20 guard hairs, although the ratio can differ by age and breed. Newborns lack primary guard hairs, hence their short and soft coats.

Types of Hairs The guard hairs make up most of the outer topcoat. They are slender, taper toward the tip, and are longer and thicker than the down or awn hairs. They protect the undercoat and act as a waterproof outer 'jacket'. Their cuticles have microscopic barbs that are very rough. The awn hairs make up the 'middle' coat. These are 'intermediate-size' hairs with rough, broken or cracked cuticles. They provide insulation and protect the down hairs underneath. The down hairs are closest to the skin and form the undercoat. They are the shortest, finest and softest hairs. Like a feather comforter, they keep the cat warm through microscopic crimps or waves that trap air. Cat hair clings to clothes because it is electrostatic and because of the guard hairs' small barbs and the awn hairs' cracked cuticles.

Vibrissae are thick, specialized hairs that are very sensitive to touch. The most apparent vibrissae hairs on the cat are its 24 whiskers arranged in four rows on each side of the muzzle. Whiskers are

more than twice as thick as ordinary hairs, and their roots are set three times deeper in a cat's tissue. Vibrissae are also found on the upper lips, the cheeks, above the eyes, and on the wrists of the forelegs.

◄ A cat does not sweat through its skin like a human, but through its paw pads and nose.

► A kitten's coat is shorter and softer than that of an adult, as the guard hairs have not yet developed.

Whiskers provide sensory information about the slightest air movement – a valuable tool for a nocturnal hunter. Cats use their whiskers in the dark to identify things they can't see, or to navigate through underbrush.

Breed Differences There is a wide variation in different breeds with regard to the size, shape and distribution of the types of hair. For example, Persians have guard hairs that are exaggerated in length. American Wirehairs have all three hair types, but all are short and curly. Cornish Rex have no guard hairs at all. While the Sphynx appears hairless, it has a light sprinkling of down hairs on some areas of its body.

Hair Growth and Shedding Cats continually shed old hair, replacing it with new live and growing hair. Anagen is the first phase during which the new hair grows beside the old hair, which is subsequently lost. Catagen is an intermediate stage, and telogen is the resting phase when the follicle becomes dormant. Different follicles are always in different phases, so the cat is never hairless.There is no such thing as a non-shedding breed. Shedding is governed by age, amount of sunlight, temperature, breed, sex, hormones, allergies and nutrition. Indoor cats who live mainly under artificial light tend to shed continuously. Strictly outdoor cats shed for several weeks during major seasonal changes, most notably spring and autumn. While the hair coat changes in appearance and texture, the number of hair follicles remains the same.

◄ Sphynx cats give the impression of being hairless, but in fact have down hairs on some parts of their bodies.

► The coat of the Devon Rex contains no guard hairs, which results in quite a different feel and texture.

Colours and Markings

There are two basic colours in cats – black and red (often referred to as orange). All other colours and patterns are the result of modifying genes that trigger changes to the basic colours.

Colours and Patterns

Solid or self-coloured A cat of one coat colour. The basic solid colours are white, black and red. White is a dominant masking gene. Although the cat has genes for other colours, white is the only colour expressed visibly. A modifying gene dilutes the colour black to blue, more commonly but incorrectly called grey. Red is diluted to cream. The chocolate modifying gene changes black into chocolate and blue into lilac, but has no effect on the red gene. Other modifying genes produce brown or cinnamon.

Parti-coloured A two-toned cat. Cats with a mix of red and black are tortoiseshells. The dilute is called blue-cream. The genes for black and red are carried on the X chromosome, often called the sex chromosome. Female cats have two X chromosomes (XX), while a normal male only has one (XY) and that is why parti-colours are females. The occasional male tortoiseshell, blue-cream or calico is the result of the male having an extra X chromosome (XXY).

Tabby A pattern, not a colour. It can be combined with any variety of other patterns and colours. Tabbies come in four main patterns. The 'mackerel' is the most common; these cats have an 'M' pattern on the forehead, striped rings around their tail and legs, a 'necklace' of stripes on the front of their chests and bands of solid or broken stripes running down the sides of their bodies. The classic or botched tabby also has the distinctive 'M' on the head but has whorls of colours ending in a 'bull's-eye' on the side of the cat and a butterfly pattern across the shoulder. The Ocicat and the American Bobtail are good examples of spotted tabby, which typically has distinct spots arranged in lines reminiscent of a mackerel tabby. Finally, a ticked tabby, such as on an Abyssinian, has hairs with distinct bands of colour on them, breaking up the patterning into a salt-and-pepper appearance. Ghost striping or 'barring' may be seen on the legs, face and belly.

Degrees of Hair Tipping

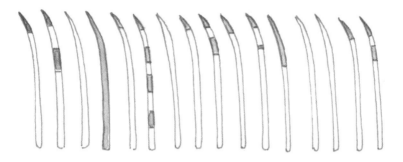

Uneven 'confused' banding – shaded type

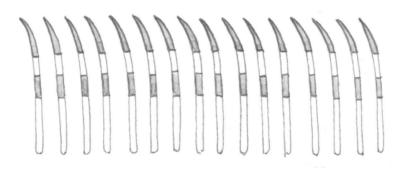

Even banding – Abssinian type ('ticked')

White

Red

Brown

Tortoiseshell-and-white (Calico)

Black

Ticked Tabby

Blue

Lilac

Mackeral Tabby

Blue-cream

Classic Tabby

Spotted Tabby

Single Spotting
Genes

Single Spotting
Genes

Two Spotting
Genes

Cinnamon

Red Point

Seal
Point

Smoke

Cream

With white (bicolour) The piebald or spotting gene adds patches of white to any other combination of colour and pattern. White spots on the chest are called lockets and white feet are known as mittens or gloves. A single spotting gene produces a cat with less than half white – often in the classical tuxedo pattern with white on the paws, chest, belly, and nose. If the cat has two spotting genes, it will be more than half white, sometimes appearing all white except for the head and tail, a pattern called van. In the Japanese Bobtail, the pattern is called Mi-Ke.

Pointed Most people are familiar with the Siamese and Himalayan cats with their striking coat pointed pattern. The pointed cat has a pale body colour with the head, tail and legs having a darker colour.

Shaded (*see* right) or Smoke This coat pattern occurs when an inhibitor gene causes colour to be confined to the tip of the hair. If the amount of colour is mostly on the tip of the hair, the colour is called 'shaded'. If the colour is more than halfway down the shaft, the cat is a smoke. If the cat is a tabby, the inhibitor changes the base colour of the tabby producing a silver tabby.

Is Colour a Breed?

Colour and pattern do not determine a cat's breed. A breed is determined by the physical characteristics described in each breed's standard, while the same colours and patterns can be seen in many different breeds. Mixed breed cats have all the same colours and patterns that are seen in purebred cats.

Different Names – Same Colour

In discussing colours of cats, it can be confusing because there are different names for the same colour. The correct term 'red' is commonly referred to as 'orange', 'rust', 'marmalade', 'yellow' and 'ginger'. Cream is often called 'buff', 'tan' or 'blonde'. Different cat registries call the same colour by different names. A calico in one organization is a 'black tortie and white' in another registry and a 'tricolour' in a third.

Sight

Because the cat is a nocturnal hunter, keen night vision was an evolutionary development that helped it become a successful predator. Contrary to popular myth, a cat cannot actually see in the dark. It can, however, see extremely well in very dim lighting conditions.

The cat's eye has several adaptations that help it see in low light. Compared to the human eye, the cat's eye is larger and rounder. Cats' eyes have more receptor cells and more neurons in the visual centres of brain.

Light passes through the cornea and pupil of the eye and strikes the retina. The cat's retina has fewer cones but more rods than the human eye. The cones perceive colour while the rods are sensitive to light. While a cat sees fewer variations in colour than a human, it sees better in low light conditions. While cats see fewer colours, they are able to distinguish more shades of grey. Since their prey species are usually

shades of grey, (mice, rats and birds) this peculiarity of vision serves them well in the wild. The cat's pupil contracts to a slit rather than a circle to give the cat more accurate control of the light entering the eye, especially in bright sunlight. The slit blocks more light than a round pupil can. Because the cats' eyelids close at right angles to the vertical pupil, the cat can further reduce the amount of light by bringing its eyelids closer together. This combination allows the cat to make very delicate adjustments and gives its vision a sharp depth of field.

◀ In darkness, a cat's pupil widens to let in as much light as possible.

Cat's Eye

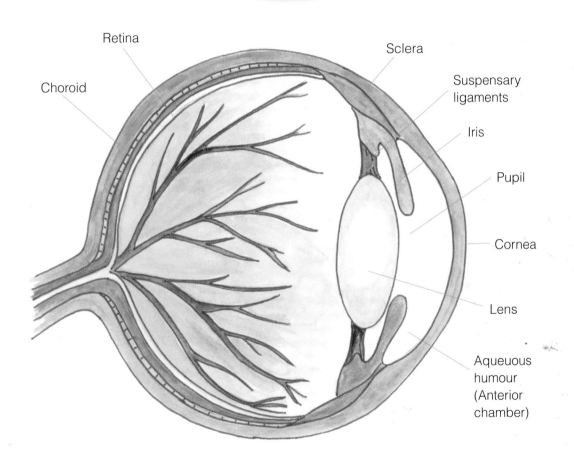

Retina

Choroid

Sclera

Suspensary
ligaments

Iris

Pupil

Cornea

Lens

Aqueuous
humour
(Anterior
chamber)

The feline's eye has an extra inner layer of cells called the tapetum lucidium that has a multiplying effect by reflecting extra light to the retina. The glow of cat's eyes in flash photography is largely due to light reflecting off the tapetum.

The eyes of the cat face forward so that the field of vision of each eye overlaps. This stereoscopic vision allows the cat to assess distance and location accurately when hunting prey. Because the eyes are deeply set in the face, the cat's field of vision is only about 185 degrees. With limited peripheral vision, the cat must turn its head to see better from side to side. Instead of the fovea that gives humans sharp central vision, cats have a central band known as the visual streak.

In addition to upper and lower eyelids, the cat has a third eyelid called the nictitating membrane or haw. The clear membrane moves across the eye as the eye moves within the socket, removing dust or debris. Lachrymal glands produce tears that wash and lubricate the eye. When a cat is sick, the third eyelid will partially close, although it is often visible in a sleepy contented cat. Because the eye is lubricated by the nictitating membrane, the cat blinks less often, an advantage when hunting in the wild.

◄ Kittens usually open their eyes at seven to ten days, but some breeds can open them in as little as two days, and occasionally a kitten is born with its eyes open.

► A cat's eyes are lubricated by the nictitating membrane, which means it needs to blink less often.

Hearing

The hearing of the cat is outstanding – even keener than that of a dog. In fact, of their six senses, a cats' hearing is the most acute. This superb hearing is an evolutionary advantage that helped cats hunt for their prey. The cat's ear consists of three sections. The external outer ear is called the pinna, or earflap. In most breeds of cats, the external ear is erect and points forward.

Thirty-two individual muscles in each ear allow it to swivel and pivot up to 180 degrees to scoop in sound waves and better pinpoint the exact source of a sound. Each ear moves independently of the other. The sound waves funnel down the ear to the eardrum that stretches across the ear canal. The middle ear has

three small bones that convert the weak sound vibrations of the eardrum into small, strong vibrations of the cochlea of the inner ear. The inner ear converts the vibrations into nerve impulses, which pass along the acoustic nerve to the brain. The cat's brain decodes the signals and recognizes them by comparing them with sounds stored in its memory bank. In this way, a cat learns to identify specific sounds. At lower-pitched frequencies, there is little difference between the hearing of cats, dogs or humans. People hear sound frequencies up to 20,000 cycles/second. Dogs hear up to 35,000 to 45,000 cycles/second. However, cats can hear sounds of an

◄ Cats have an amazing ability to distinguish between sounds, although loud noises can frighten them.

► A cat's ears can move independently of each other and can swivel up to 180 degrees to aid sound location.

amazingly high pitch – up to 100,000 cycles/second. That is two octaves above what humans can hear and includes ultrasonic sound waves. It is also the high-pitched range of sounds made by mice and other small rodents – the food source for a cat when in the wild.

Cats are expert at telling the precise direction from which a sound originates. The cat determines the direction of the source of the sound by differences in the time of arrival and intensity of sound received by each ear. A cat can differentiate between two sound sources separated by as little an angle as 5 degrees. At a distance of 60 feet, a cat can distinguish between two sounds that are only 18 inches apart. A cat can tell the difference between two sounds from the same direction but at different distances. Their keen hearing even makes it possible for the cat to distinguish between very similar sounds. In a crowded show hall filled with people and other felines, a cat can distinguish the sound of its owner's footsteps.

The cats' ability to hear even the faintest noise can sometimes be a concern in a noisy situations. A cat may be upset by the noise of a vacuum cleaner or loud music or outdoor noises such as a lawn mower or traffic.

Smell, Taste and Touch

Its sense of smell is perhaps the most important of the cat's senses because it is critical to its hunting, feeding and sexual behaviour. A cat's sense of smell is about 14 times that of a human's. The cat has approximately 60 to 80 million olfactory cells that gather and identify the most delicate and subtle scents. By comparison, a human has only 5 to 20

◄ A cat's sense of smell is vital to many facets of its life.

Cat Olfactory System

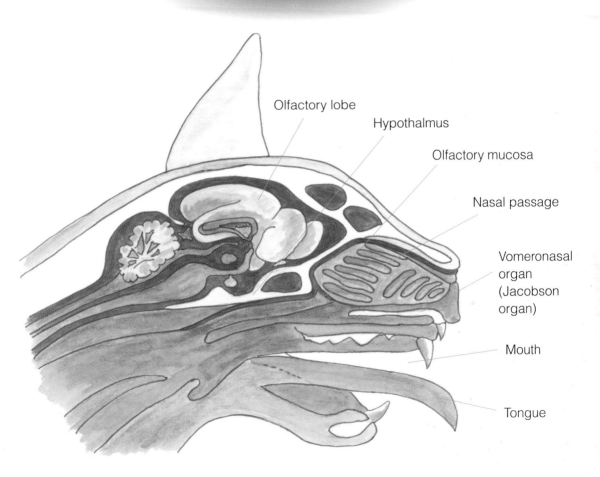

Olfactory lobe

Hypothalmus

Olfactory mucosa

Nasal passage

Vomeronasal organ (Jacobson organ)

Mouth

Tongue

million olfactory cells, which means cats smell things of which we are not aware. Even the olfactory region of the cat's brain is larger than expected.

The Flehmen Reaction

Cats have a specialized scent organ located in the roof of the mouth just behind the front teeth. Called the vomeronasal sac or Jacobson's organ, it is a small pouch lined with receptor cells and connects to the nasal cavity. When a cat smells certain scents, especially musky or sexual ones, it stretches its neck, opens its mouth, and curls its upper lip. This is termed the Flehmen Reaction. The tongue gathers minute particles of scent and then is pressed to the roof of the mouth, transferring the scent molecules to the Jacobson's organ. Opening the mouth slightly enables the ducts to open up connecting to the nasal cavity. The appearance of the cat as it brings air into the Jacobson's organ looks like a smile or a grimace.

Taste

It is not unusual for a cat owner to be surprised by the sandpaper kiss of a cat. What makes the cat's tongue so rough is the numerous hard projections called papillae on the surface. The papillae form backward-facing hooks containing large amounts of keratin, the same material found in human fingernails. The hardness and strength of these hooks helps the cat hold prey. The hooks also provide the abrasiveness that is so effective when a cat grooms itself.

◄ Cats drink by making their tongues into a spoon-like shape and flicking liquid into their mouths.

► The rough surface of a cat's tongue is covered in hard, backward-facing hooks called papillae.

The cat has two sets of taste buds. The ones on the tip and the sides of the tongue are mushroom-shaped papillae that contain some of the largest taste buds. At the very front of the tongue are smaller, circular 'fungiform' papillae. These two sets of taste buds make a cat's sense of taste extremely sensitive. In 2005, it was discovered that the cat family lacks the T1R2 protein, one of two proteins necessary to taste sweetness. Most scientists believe this mutation may have led to the cat's role as a strict carnivore. Their modified sense of taste would cause them to ignore plants, a large part of whose taste appeal derives from their high sugar content. Instead, the cats favor of a high-protein carnivorous diet, which stimulates their taste receptors.

In addition to flavour, a cat's tongue is sensitive to the texture or 'mouth feel' of a particular food. The cat's tongue also reacts to temperature, preferring foods at room temperature.

Water is an essential ingredient and is involved in virtually every function of a cat's body. A cat drinks by making its tongue into a spoon shape. It flicks its tongue quickly in and out of the water, swallowing after

every third or fourth lap. A cat's water intake will vary depending on the air temperature and humidity, the cat's activity level and its diet. Cats fed canned cat food with its high moisture content will not drink as much water as those eating dry food.

Sense of Touch

Like humans, cats have touch receptors all over their body that transfer sensations of pressure, temperature and pain from nerve cells to the brain. The most sensitive places on the cat's body are the face and front paws. These are the body parts the cat uses most while hunting. The skin of the pads on the underside of a cat's paw is

sensitive to pressure, but not to a delicate touch. It is the hairs on the tip of the paw that are very sensitive – not the pads.

The nose leather (the fleshy part of the nose) is also very sensitive to touch. It is also receptive to temperature and humidity – like a barometer.

The cat's whiskers also play a critical role in sensation. A cat has about 24 moveable vibrissae or whiskers in four rows on each upper lip on each side of its muzzle in addition to a few on each cheek, tufts over the eyes, bristles on the chin, the inner forelegs and at the back of the legs.

Richly supplied with nerve endings at their base, whiskers give cats extraordinarily detailed information about air movements, air pressure and anything they touch. The upper two rows of whiskers can move independently from the lower two rows for precise measuring. As air swirls around objects, whiskers vibrate, detecting very small shifts in air currents. This enables a cat to sense the presence, size and shape of obstacles without seeing or touching them – a great advantage when hunting in the dark. The structure of the area of the brain region, which receives information from the vibrissae, is similar to that found in the visual cortex, implying a cat's perception through its whiskers is similar to seeing. When a cat's prey is too near for accurate vision, its whiskers move to form a basket shape around its muzzle to

detect the prey's location. A cat may rely on the whiskers in dim light where fully dilating the pupils would reduce its ability to focus on close objects. The whiskers also spread out roughly as wide as the cat's body making it able to judge if it can fit through an opening.

◀ Cats can use their whiskers to help them locate other animals when they are too near to see them accurately.

▶ A cat's nose leather is very sensitive and responds to changes in temperature and humidity.

Cat Behaviour

'**Thousands of years ago, cats were worshipped as gods.** Cats have never forgotten this' ... (author unknown). Feline behaviour has intrigued humans for centuries, probably because much of the domesticated cat's behaviour reflects the patterns inherited from its wild ancestors. This is part of the charm and mystique of the cat. Gaining an insight into how and why a cat reacts to its environment is sure to enhance the owner's enjoyment and appreciation of their pet. Many things that a cat does in its home are simply extensions of instinctive habits from the wild.

Cat Psychology

The Catnap and Nocturnal Activity

The average cat sleeps for 13–18 hours a day. Newborn kittens sleep almost non-stop. This is an instinctive behaviour that protects them in the wild, as while they are asleep they cannot wander away from the nest. Sleeping, the kittens also make no noise that might attract a predator. As the kittens grow, their proportion of sleeping to time awake gradually changes until they attain typical adult sleep patterns. Like people, cats will sleep more as they enter old age.

About one-third of a cat's sleeping time is spent in a deep sleep during which it may dream. Twitching muscles, meows and growls and purrs, often accompany dreams. Unlike humans, cats spend many hours sleeping relatively lightly. During light sleep, the body temperature lowers slightly, the muscles are slightly tensed, and the blood pressure remains normal. A cat can go from a light sleep to being fully

awake instantly. Because a cat in the wild is a nocturnal hunter, some cats will tend to sleep all day and then wander the house at night.

A cat can sleep anywhere but prefers a sleeping place that feels safe. Some cats like to be up high and choose a shelf in a cupboard. Some prefer enclosed spaces like under the sofa. During hot summer days, a cat may prefer the cool porcelain of bathroom sink. In the winter, most cats cosy up to a warm spot near a radiator. Temperature also affects the cat's sleeping position. When cold, cats tend to curl in a ball and put their face between their paws to reduce body heat loss. When hot they will sleep stretched out with the belly turned upward to release the body heat.

The Catnip Response

Catnip (*Nepetia cataria*) is a plant native to North America. Fresh leaves of the catnip plant have a mint-like scent while dried leaves smell like alfalfa. Watching a cat respond to catnip amuses most people. Pawing, clasping, rolling onto the side and rhythmic kicking with the back feet is behaviour similar to that displayed when they detect and capture prey. Some cats enjoy catnip and seem to revel in its effects, while other cats appear to avoid it, despite prior displays of catnip sensitivity. Generally, male and female cats of reproductive age are more sensitive to catnip than very young or old cats. Catnip is not toxic to pets.

◀ Some cats respond to catnip, while others remain unaffected.

Inappropriate Biting

Just like human babies, kittens have the urge to chew and bite when they are teething. Or a cat may scratch or bite without warning when you are petting it as a result of over-stimulation. To correct either situation, distract the cat with a toy that is a more acceptable object for aggression.

Poor Litter Tray Habits

If a previously clean cat begins scratching outside the litter tray, this is a signal the cat is not happy about something. It may be that the tray needs to be cleaned or it is displeased with the feel of the litter; the smell of the litter; the type of tray or even the location of the tray.

Clawing Furniture

Contrary to popular belief, when a cat claws the furniture, it is not sharpening its claws. Scratching helps the cat remove the old claw sheath to expose the new, sharp ones. Cats also scratch on objects to mark their territory by stimulating the release of a scent from glands located between the paw pads.

◄ Toys can be used to distract cats that bite during petting.

► Cats scratch to remove old claw sheaths and to scent-mark territory.

▲ Cats can be distracted from the desire to ambush
their owners by providing them with a playmate.

Kneading

Young kittens instinctively knead their mother's nipples with their tiny forepaws while nursing. The kneading stimulates the flow of milk. When a kitten kneads the lap of his owner, it is mirroring the same happiness that it felt nursing at its mother's belly. While most people recognize and appreciate the privilege a cat bestows when kneading on their person, if the kneading is uncomfortable, too enthusiastic or continues too long, the cat can be gently discouraged by simply distracting it. Keeping the cat's nails clipped short helps too.

Burying Food

If a cat does not like the taste of wet food on a plate, it may try to 'bury' it by scratching repeatedly at the floor or covering it up with whatever might be nearby – a mat, bed or toy. Even if the cat likes the food, if there is more than it can eat at one meal, it will scrape its paw along the floor as if covering the food. This is an instinctive behaviour left over from when a wild cat would bury the remains of a kill to eat later.

Running Water

The sound and motion of water pouring from a tap is mesmerizing to many cats. It is quite likely a feast for the senses as it stimulates hearing, sight, smell and touch. Many cats prefer to drink from a running tap as the water is fresh. Water that has been standing even a few hours loses some of its oxygen content, and that changes its taste.

The Foot Attack

Even the most domesticated cat may feel the urge to practise its predatory skills. Some cats make up elaborate prey games, hiding underneath furniture or behind a door waiting for their person to stroll by, then leaping out and attacking their feet. The cat is not trying to hurt you but is simply reacting to an instinctive urge to hunt. The cat can be discouraged by providing it with more playtime or providing it with a feline playmate.

Retrieving

In the wild, when a cat takes down prey, it will often carry it to a safe spot to consume it. The indoor cat's equivalent of this behaviour is to retrieving objects in the manner of a dog playing fetch.

Sucking, Nursing or Chewing on Materials

Thought to be a behaviour more common if a kitten has been weaned too early, some cats will suck or nurse on material or objects. While some kittens outgrow the behaviour, putting something on the item that

is distasteful to the cat, such as paprika, cologne or a citrus scent can discourage the behaviour. Some cats seem unable to resist chewing on photos or paper. Some people believe that some cats detect a slight odour, or that the coolness and texture of the plastic feels and tastes good on the cat's tongue.

A related activity is called 'pica', it is an abnormal compulsion to eat things that are not usually eaten. While rare, some cats, particularly the Oriental breeds, are noted for snacking on everything from sweaters to phone cords.

Instinct and Learning

The size of the average cat brain is 5 cm (2 in) in length and 30 g (1 oz) in weight. Since the average cat weighs about 3.3 kg (7 lb), the brain is less than 0.9 per cent of its total body weight, compared with the average human's brain which accounts for two per cent of its body weight.

Cats learn by trial and error, observation and imitation. The cat's learning abilities are aided by an excellent memory. Cats can remember and recall information much longer than dogs – up to 16 hours as opposed to a dog's five minutes. In one study, it was discovered that cats possess visual memory ability comparable to that of monkeys. The feline short-term working memory is less impressive however. One study showed that dogs were better than cats in short-term memory tests.

While a cat is born with strong instincts, its aptitude for gathering and analyzing information and learning through experience serves it well. A kitten first learns by imitating its mother. As it grows more independent, it does something, and then observes the results. If an action is pleasant, it is likely to repeat it. If not, it will be less likely to do it again.

A kitten can be seen imitating hunting behaviour very early, at about one month old. If it is an outside cat, the mother will bring prey, dead or alive, by the time the kitten is six weeks old. By two months of age the kitten will have

◀ Cats learn about cleanliness from their mother and will use a litter tray from the age of five to six weeks.

learned how to hunt and by six months it will be a confident hunter capable of satisfying its needs. all by imitating its mother.

The kitten is also taught hygiene and cleanliness by its mother. The mother keeps the birth nest clean by licking and eating the urine and faeces of her nursing kittens. As a kitten starts to walk and starts to eat solid food, the mother cat will no longer clean the kitten's bottom. A kitten will not soil its own bed and will use a litter tray by the time it is five to six weeks old, if it is made readily available.

The mother cat is constantly grooming her newborn kittens and the kitten imitates her licking behaviour. Like a human baby, a kitten explores its environment by putting things in its mouth. This is how it learns what is food and what is not. It is trial and error combined with watching what its mother eats.

Territoriality

In the wild cats are territorial. The male stakes out a territory as his food source. He will also protect the area for his female and his kittens. A male may even attack and kill young kittens sired by another male to eliminate competition.

Cats mark their territory by spraying concentrated urine. While usually associated with tom cats, whole females and some neutered males will exhibit spraying behaviour.

◄ A tom cat marks his territory by spraying concentrated urine on some shrubbery.

► Cats have scent glands on the sides and back of their heads, which they rub on things to mark ownership.

A cat will re-mark its territory if the previous scent markers have been washed away by weather or cleaning. The usual reason for a previously clean cat to begin urine-marking indoors is a reaction to stress. Commonly, the introduction of a new cat to the household will upset a cat. Feeling threatened or stressed by the presence of the strange cat, the resident feline will mark the home as 'his'.

The cat has glands that secrete scents in several areas of its body but particularly concentrated around the sides and back of the head. When a cat rubs its head along your legs it is marking you – sending a message that you belong to it. Similarly, the cat will rub on furniture in the home. The outdoor cat will rub against walls, fences, bushes and trees.

Marking trees with its claws is another message a cat leaves to be interpreted by other felines. The higher the marks, the larger and more dominant the cat that made the marks, so a cat stretches as far up as it can when scratching on a tree. When the cat digs its claws into the tree it also leaves a scent message from glands between the paw pads.

Curiosity and the Cat

The cat is fabled for its inexhaustible curiosity. Its inquisitiveness is the result of the mixture of its lively intelligence, highly tuned senses, and its evolutionary instincts as a predator.

▶ Cats are well known for their curiosity and they cannot resist peeking into nooks and crannies.

Movement and Balance

Generally, the size and shape of the average domestic cat has remained relatively constant throughout its association with man. Whether sprinting after prey or stalking in slow motion, the cat is built for speed and coordination. A cat in good shape can run 48 kph (30 mph). The cat is a sprinter, however, and not a long-distance runner.

Cats are digitigrades: they walk directly on their toes. Cats are capable of walking very precisely because they place each hind paw almost directly in the print of the corresponding forepaw, minimizing noise and visible tracks and providing sure footing. The cat, the giraffe, and the camel are the only mammals that walk by moving the front and hind legs first on one side, then the other.

A cat is able to jump more than five times its own height in a single leap. When preparing for a jump, the cat observes closely the place it intends to jump to, calculating the distance and exact angle before making the leap. Like Nijinsky, the cat then jumps with style and elegance no matter the distance, the tail acting to balance the cat in the air. Seldom does a cat injure itself, even when the jumps are very large or a landing miscalculated.

Jumping downwards is a little trickier. Most cats try to shorten the distance they have to jump by putting their front paws as close as possible to their target, and then pushing off with their hind legs.

▲ A cat's tail is essential for balancing, whilst jumping.

The Self-righting Reflex

Perhaps one of the most unique feline characteristics is a cat's innate ability to right itself and land on its feet when falling from a height. While not infallible, a falling cat is usually able to twist itself around to land on its paws. This is called the self-righting reflex. A kitten begins to demonstrate the righting reflex at three to four weeks of age, and usually perfects it by seven weeks old.

The vestibular apparatus of the inner ear of the cat contains three semicircular canals. Like a carpenter's level, these structures work with the brain to sense and maintain balance. When a cat falls with its legs higher than its body, impulses from the vestibular apparatus are analysed at lightening speed and combine with visual information to transmit a message to the cat's neck muscles to orient correctly.

Because the cat has a highly flexible spine and floating collarbone, the head is able to twist into an upright, horizontal position, independent of the rest of the body. Next, the front feet rotate until they are facing the ground.

◀ These images show the series of movements by which a cat can right itself while falling from a height.

▶ Many cats can climb trees fairly easily, but coming down is not so easy, sometimes resulting in falls.

Finally the hind legs swivel around until the cat has completely righted itself in mid-air.

The hind legs touch down first, relaxing to act as shock absorbers. The spine arches to further minimize impact and the front legs relax to lessen the possibility of injury. Like a skydiver, a falling cat will reach a point in its fall where it is no longer accelerating. This is termed terminal or maximum velocity. The average cat reaches a speed of 100 km/h (60 ml/h) after falling about five storeys. Small size, light bone structure, thick fur and spreading the legs out to increase drag all contribute to slowing down the descent.

Once a cat has righted itself, reached maximum velocity, and is no longer receiving the stimuli to right itself, it goes into 'free-fall' and relaxes. The relaxed cat is less likely to sustain injury as it lands.

Self-Grooming

If there were an animal Olympics for self-grooming, the cat would win the gold medal. Cats are enthusiastic self-groomers, spending a great deal of their waking hours grooming. So addictive is the grooming behaviour, that after thoroughly washing itself, a cat will often attempt to groom a companion, whether

another cat, a human or the family dog. Mother cats are dedicated to the washing of their kittens. It is not unusual to hear a young kitten squeal in protest as 'mum' holds it down and licks, licks, licks. A cat may groom meticulously after being petted, possibly in an attempt to remove the scent of the person who touched it.

◄ Cats clean their paws meticulously in an effort to remove anything caught between their pads.

► Cats will often wash a companion when they have completed their own grooming.

Anyone having experienced the rough kiss of the family cat realizes that the feline tongue is not smooth. It is in fact covered with hard, strong, backward facing hooks called papillae that are well suited to cleaning the cat's coat. Acting like a comb, the tongue removes dirt, oils and loose hair as it licks the coat. The cat will use its tongue to lick all the parts it can reach. A grooming session typically begins with a thorough licking from shoulder to flank followed by the underside, tail and hind legs. Special attention is paid to cleaning around the anus and genital regions. Paws are inspected, biting any debris that may be stuck in the hair between the pads.

Once the cat has groomed all the areas it can reach with its tongue directly, it moves on to grooming the difficult to reach areas like the face and behind the ears. Assuming a sitting position, the cat will continuously lick the inside of a front paw and leg until it is wet. It then rubs the wet paw along the side of its face and cheeks, around the eye, the forehead and behind the ear. Once it completely cleans the side of its head, it changes paws and repeats the procedure on the other side of its face.

So efficient is the abrasive tongue at removing dead hair from the coat, the cat often ingests so much loose hair that it forms a ball in the cat's stomach. Unable to pass through the digestive tract, the cat usually vomits up the ball of hair. If the hair does enter the intestine, there is a danger it may become impacted in the gastrointestinal tract. This is one reason why it is important to comb your cat frequently, especially during shedding season. Longhaired cats need daily grooming. Shorthaired cats should be groomed once a week.

◄ During a thorough grooming session a cat works its way around its body, cleaning each area in detail.

► Cats usually assume a seated position for cleaning the face and ears.

Hunting

Despite centuries of domestication, most cats display an instinct to hunt if given the opportunity. This predatory behaviour has been passed down to the domestic cat through the mists of time. While cats are born with a hunting instinct, killing and eating prey are generally learned behaviours. While a cat may catch and kill a mouse, it might not eat it even if it is hungry, unless it has been taught to.

Kittens begin to show hunting behaviour as young as six weeks of age. Programmed from birth to chase, kittens practise hunting skills by crouching, pouncing, play fighting and mock-attacking with their littermates.

A mother cat might use her tail to help teach her babies hunting skills by using it as a 'tease' to teach them to stalk. If the mother is an outdoor cat, she will bring small dead prey to her kittens. She will eat in front of them, encouraging them to join her. Next, she will bring injured prey and encourage her kittens to

◀ Kittens are taught to hunt by their mother and begin to practise their skills from an early age.

▶ Most domestic cats retain the hunting instinct, although not all kill and eat their prey.

play with it. She will kill it in front of them. Slowly, the kittens learn that prey can be caught and eaten. Eventually, the kittens accompany the mother as she hunts and learn to catch and kill on their own.

Cats will exhibit teaching behaviour not only towards their own kittens but other cat's litters. Some cats even include their human owners in the lesson, bringing home dead prey and dropping it on the doorstep. The hunting feline patrols a specific territory. The size of the territory varies depending on the availability of prey. Most adults are solitary hunters although at times cats hunt in cooperation.

The cat kills with a lethal bite through the spinal at the base of the neck. If a cat isn't hungry, it will delay or even defer killing the prey, instead opting for the excitement of repeated stalking, capturing, and playing with the victim.

Why do cats often appear to torture or play with their catch before killing it? There are several theories. One theory is that these cats lack confidence. They may still be wary of their prey, which if not killed quickly can fight and bite back. Another theory is that domestic cats that live in a relatively rodent-free environment lack the opportunity to catch real live prey. When they finally do catch a mouse, they want to prolong the 'great' event as much as possible. 'Birding' is a distinctive teeth chattering sort of noise that some cats seem to reserve for when they see birds or squirrels or feathers. Indoor cats may just be showing their excitement or frustration at seeing potential prey that they cannot reach.

Communication

Cats communicate by smell, vocalizing, body language and marking.

Vocalizations

Cats have a wide range of vocalizations that include murmurs, meows, spitting, hisses and growls. These can be divided into three broad categories: closed mouth, vowel patterns and intense vocalizations patterns.

Purring, mating vocalizations, and the closed-mouth 'mrrrr?' uttered when a cat seems to be asking a question are closed mouth vocalizations. Vowel patterns include the more typical 'meow' and are produced when the cat opens and closes its mouth when making the sound. Cats meow for various reasons but most often because they want something like food, petting, attention or to go outside. Intense vocalizations are produced when the cat holds the mouth open throughout the sound, usually when aroused, demanding or upset. These include growling, hissing and screaming. Some cats are 'talkers', meowing repeatedly or for an extended period especially in responds to the human voice. Oriental breeds such as the Siamese, are renowned for being chatty.

Purring Part of the admiration humans feel for the feline is its unique ability to purr. Small cats, including the domestic cat, purr on both the inhaled and exhaled breath. The big cats purr only when they breathe out. Cats can purr with their mouths tightly closed. Kittens are born blind and deaf yet purr in response to their mother licking them. Kittens can purr with their mother's nipple in their mouth. Because a kitten cannot nurse and meow at the same time, it purrs while nursing to let its mother know all is well. Their mother purrs so that they can find her, and purring acts to comfort both of them. Kittens do not purr in response to human touch until about six weeks old.

▶ Cats can meow for a number of reasons, but it often indicates that they want food or attention.

This phenomenon of suckling and purring at the same time can occur because purring is not a vocal sound. The purr does not come from the true vocal cords. No one really knows for sure where the purr sound comes from although there are several theories on the subject. Cats purr when they are happy but also purr when in pain. Pain stimulates the hypothalamus to release endorphins to help block the pain. But perhaps it doesn't really matter how a cat purrs, or why it purrs. It is enough that they do purr.

Body Language

Cats easily convey their feelings through body language. Everyone recognizes the raised back and flattened ears of a frightened feline.

Expressive Ears A cat's ears are used for more than just hearing. The angle of a cat's ears is an important clue to its mood. If the ears prick forward, the cat is showing interest. Ears pointed to the side mean the cat is thinking and considering its next move. If the ears are plastered flat against its head, look out, the cat is not happy. Ears back and down indicate fear.

Tail Talk Besides contributing to a cat's overall beauty and balance, the tail tells about the cat's emotional state. The way your cat holds its tail and each movement of the tail communicates what it is thinking and feeling. You just need to learn how to speak 'talk tail'. Held erect for its full length, the tail is used as a greeting. If the tail is held erect and gently

◄ An erect tail with the tip tilted over indicates that a cat is feeling friendly but has slight reservations.

► The forward-held ears of this cat indicate that it is alert and interested in something.

quivering, the cat is displaying affection. If the tail is erect, but tip is tilted over, this means the cat is in a friendly mood but has slight reservations. If the tail is held upright but curved to one side, it indicates a desire to play. The tail straight up is a request for food. If the tail is raised slightly and softly curved, the cat is beginning to be interested in something. If the tail is curved over the cat's back, it means it is expecting something to happen.

If the tail is fully lowered and tucked between the hind legs, it indicates the cat is feeling submissive. If the tail is lowered and still, but the tip is twitching slightly, the cat is feeling mildly irritated. If the tail is wrapped around the cat's body, it usually indicates that the cat is contented although sometimes it can be the defensive posture of a nervous cat.

If the tail waves slowly and gently to and fro it indicates pleasure. The tail flicks of a seated cat indicate irritation or indecision. A tail tip of a cat quivers when excited. A tail that wags back and forth, then pauses, and repeats the sequence is annoyed. A tail slashing back and forth in wide arcs means the cat is angry and you'd better watch out.

If the tail is arched over the back and puffed up, the cat is feeling defensive. If the tail is puffed up and held straight up and the back is arched, the cat is feeling aggressive and may be ready to attack. If the tail is lowered and fluffed the cat is fearful. Tail held to one side by a female cat indicates that the female is in season and inviting a sexual advance.

Scent

Cats recognize one another by their scent. Scent glands called temporal glands are situated above the eyes on the sides of the forehead. Cats mark objects including people they consider 'theirs' by rubbing the side of their heads along their object of affection. Cats mark their territory with urine. Other cats smell the urine and recognize the message.

Getting ready for your
Cat

Getting A New Cat

The cat is a special creature, beautiful and elegant in form, with mystery in its eyes and music in its purr. The unconditional love and companionship provided by owning a cat is enjoyed by millions of happy owners around the world. When you decide to invite a cat to be part of your life, you will be rewarded with a lifelong friend, but the decision to adopt a kitten is not one to be entered into lightly.

Points to Consider

Like a happy marriage, sharing your life with a cat requires careful planning and preparation beforehand to be a success. With modern advances in veterinary medicine, it is not unusual to see a cat enjoying good health into its late teens and twenties. Thus, welcoming a feline member into the family is a major commitment and responsibility, and not a step to be taken impulsively. While the cute kitten in the cardboard box with a sign 'free to a good home' seems like a bargain, before you let your heart rule your head, first consider the financial costs of owning a cat. The cost of maintenance of your kitten will vary depending on where you live, so investigate the cost of products and services in your area. Things to consider include:

Food Choose a good quality cat food formulated for kittens.

Litter tray and Litter A simple litter tray is not expensive. Factor in the cost of litter.

Spay or Neutering There will be a one-off expense to spay or neuter the kitten.

Vaccinations The kitten will require a series of vaccinations for Feline Enteritis, Calici, Rhinotracheitis and Rabies plus yearly boosters.

Worming A faecal check will determine if your kitten needs to be wormed.

Annual Checkup When your cat goes to the vet for its annual booster vaccinations, it should receive a thorough checkup, including a dental and blood profile.

Dental Care A cat may require regular yearly teeth cleaning, especially as it enters middle age.

Emergency Veterinary Care No one can predict if your cat might have a health crisis but you should have money available to pay unexpected veterinary fees.

Pet Insurance Pet health insurance is an option to consider to ease the financial burden of veterinary care.

Boarding If you frequently go on holidays or business trips, and must board the cat, investigate the costs of an appropriate facility.

Once you have tallied up the approximate costs and are confident that you can afford to have a cat join your family, next consider how a kitten will fit into your home life.

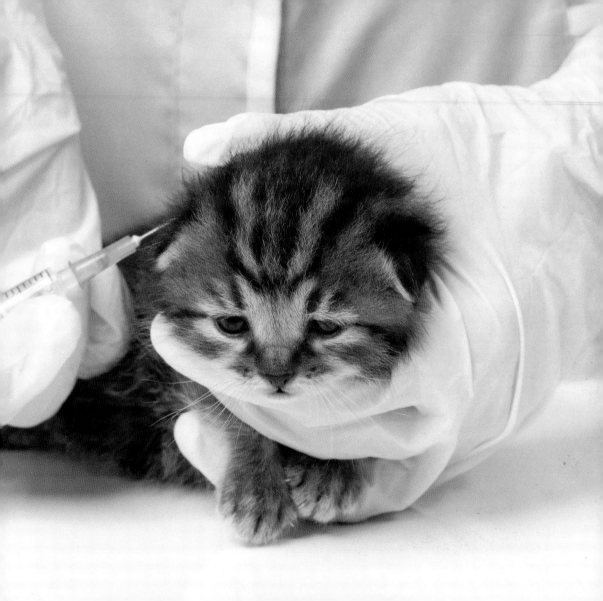

If you have children, are they old enough to understand how to treat a cat properly? Who in the family will have the responsibility of caring for the cat? Even if you hope to teach children responsibility by assigning to them some of the 'kitty chores', an adult should supervise. How do other members of the family feel about getting a cat? Do you have other pets and how will they adjust to a new cat?

Do you have the time to spend with a cat? Contrary to popular opinion, most cats need and enjoy attention. A neglected cat is more likely to get into mischief just to relieve the boredom. You may wonder if you have room for a cat. If there is enough room for you, there is enough for a cat. The cat in a huge mansion is no happier than the cat in a small flat on the twentieth floor of a tower block – as long as both are well loved.

Choosing Your Cat

Once you are sure a cat is the right pet for you, there are more decisions to be made before you actually go looking for that special feline. Do not be seduced into purchasing an appealing kitten on the spur of

the moment. Consider your lifestyle and preferences before choosing a healthy, well-socialized kitten with the needs, temperament and personality that best suit you and your family.

Male or Female

If you do not intend to become a cat breeder, the sex of your kitten is immaterial to its role as a family pet. While

◀ As long as a cat is well loved and looked after, the size and location of its residence is unimportant.

some people swear male cats are more affectionate, others passionately prefer a female. The truth is that since most kittens are neutered or spayed by six months of age, there really is not a lot of difference between the sexes. It is far more important to look for the right personality, rather than limiting your choice based on the sex of the kitten.

Mixed Breed or Pedigreed

'Moggies' is an English slang term for a domestic cat of unknown parentage. mixed-breed kittens are readily available and less expensive than a pedigreed cat. When choosing a moggie, the only drawback is that you have little information about its medical or genetic history, so have a veterinary examination before losing your heart to a kitten that may have a major health issue. On the other

hand, you may have fallen in love with a particular breed's look and personality. Perhaps you are considering showing your cat or eventually breeding it. The advantage of a purebred, more correctly called a pedigreed cat, is that it is more of a known quantity. It offers predictability. While cats are individuals and will vary, cats of the same breed are likely to share the look and personality traits characteristic of its breed. Seek out a reputable breeder who has carefully chosen quality breeding stock and is skilled at raising and socializing kittens. Many breeders provide expert advice to their kitten buyers long after the original purchase.

◄ While mixed-breed kittens cost less and are easier to find, more information may be available for pedigrees.

Kitten or Adult

The appeal of a kitten is difficult to resist. While a kitten requires an enormous amount of time and care, it is compensated by the delight of watching it grow and develop. However, an older cat may be a better choice if you lead a hectic lifestyle or have children under three years of age who may be too young to be trusted to treat a kitten gently.

▲ There are always many adult cats in need of good homes, for a wide variety of reasons.

For various reasons, a new home might be needed for an adult cat due to divorce, allergies, a change in family circumstances or a pedigreed cat may be retiring from a breeding career. Grown cats have the advantage of maturity, are already vaccinated and neutered. There is also the satisfaction of providing a home to a cat that, but for you, may never find a home since people naturally gravitate toward kittens. One caveat; adult cats in shelters may have been turned in due to behavioural problems, typically poor litter tray habits. If selecting an adult cat from a shelter try to determine the reason its last home gave it up.

Special-Needs Feline

You might want to consider adopting a special-needs cat, one that is blind, an amputee or has a health problem that is manageable with medication such as diabetes. Often labelled unadoptable, opening your heart and home to a special-needs feline is rewarded with love and companionship that more than compensates for the extra care that may be required.

▶ Giving a home to a special-needs feline, such as this one-eyed cat, can be a rewarding experience.

Longhair or Shorthair

The grooming requirements of a longhaired cat such as a Persian are significant. Even a mixed breed with semi-longhair will require regular combing to avoid matting. A shorthair requires less grooming but the shed hair may be more difficult to remove from clothes and furniture.

One Cat or Two

Two cats are more than twice the fun and less than twice the work. Once you have adjusted your lifestyle to accommodate one cat, adopting another requires little extra. It is not unusual for someone to go to a shelter or a breeder to adopt one kitty and to come home with two. The kittens maybe so adorable you cannot choose between them, so you decide to take both. Two cats are very entertaining as they play and interact with one another, adding an extra portion of fun to the home.

A Reputable Breeder

If purchasing a pedigreed cat, it is best to buy directly from a reputable breeder. Cat breeders can be located through cat clubs, visiting a local cat show, advertisements or on the internet. When you purchase a pet kitten from a breeder who shows their cats, the pet kitten has received all the extra care, nutrition and attention to genetics as the show kitten in the same litter. Most breeders offer a contract with a written guarantee, although the conditions of the contract may vary. If you have purchased a pedigreed kitten as a pet from a breeder, there are generally two possibilities regarding registration papers. The breeder will either give you the pink and/or blue slips signed 'Not for Breeding' and

▶ Longhaired cats require more grooming, but hairs from shorthaired cats tend to get everywhere.

'Spay/Neuter', or they will withhold the papers until they have received your veterinarian's confirmation that the kitten has been spayed or neutered. With the papers in hand, you can then register your kitten.

Not all private breeders are reputable and the informed buyer should interview breeders to separate the good ones from the bad. The term 'Back Yard Breeder' or BYB is used to describe a breeder whose primary motivation is making a profit, often resulting in producing substandard, unhealthy kittens.

Feline and Breed Rescues

Feline or breed rescue groups are typically staffed by volunteers and funded by donations. Most depend on volunteer foster homes to care for the cats until a permanent home can be located. Foster homes assess the cat's health and behaviour, providing medical care and remedial training if necessary before offering the cat for rehoming. You can often find a pedigreed cat from a breed rescue for a significantly lower price than from a breeder. You must pass a rigorous screening test before you will be approved as a prospective home.

'Free to a Good Home'

If you are looking for a mixed-breed kitten, word of mouth or a classified advertisement may lead you to someone with kittens to give away, unfortunately usually the result of failure to spay an outdoor cat. Question the owner about the kitten's history, whether it's had vaccinations, and any illness in the litter. Ask to see the mother cat in her home

environment to evaluate her temperament. You'll also get a better idea of the conditions the kitten has been living in, whether there is any indication of illness in the rest of the litter, and the condition of the mother cat.

Humane or Animal Shelters

With the exception of a no-kill shelter, kittens and cats at a humane society are almost always destined for euthanasia if not adopted. Adopt a cat or kitten and you may be saving a life. The drawback is that you will have little information about the kitten's medical or genetic background. Shelters charge an adoption fee, which often includes vaccinations and neutering.

Pet Stores

Pet stores are the place to buy food and accessories for your cat, but not an ideal place for the purchase of a kitten. Most pet stores get their animals from 'kitten mills'– commercial operations breeding for profit, and not to preserve or promote specific traits of the breed. There is some risk as to whether such kittens will be of good temperament or health as the parents cannot be seen and often little or no information is available regarding their background or breeding. Some large chain stores, such as PetSmart in the US, have arrangements with local rescue groups to allow showing of their rescued cats, usually on weekends.

▶ Adopting a cat or kitten from a shelter may incur a small fee to cover neutering and vaccinations.

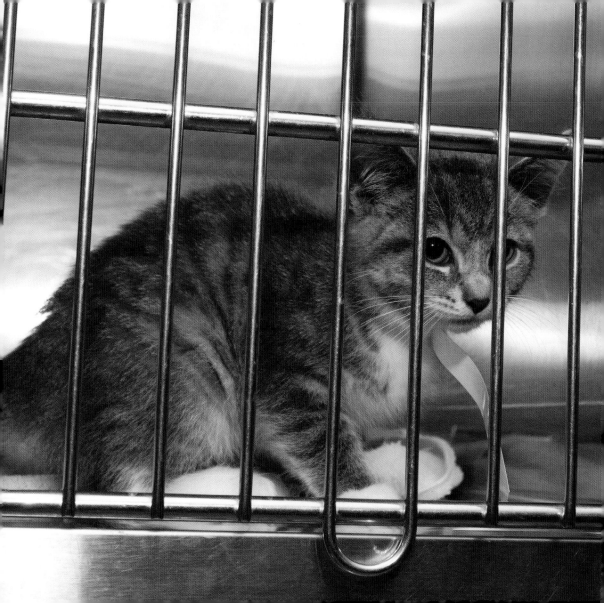

Your Cat's Environment

Part of the excitement of adopting a new kitten is the preparation that goes into getting the house ready for the new arrival. Before you bring your new kitten home, there are preparations to complete, things to buy, decisions to be made. Firstly, what are you going to bring the kitten home in? Then, where will it sleep? How often will it need grooming? And what will happen when you go on holiday? These are just a few of the questions we will help you answer.

The New Home

Carriers

For the safety of your cat, always travel with it in a carrier. Carriers come in several styles. The most economical is a simple cardboard carrier, often available from your vet or pet shop. Hard

◄ Plastic carriers are long lasting, easy to clean and provide a secure environment for a frightened cat.

plastic or fibreglass carriers last longer, are more secure, easily cleaned and disinfected, and fold away for convenient storage. They are warm and cosy and provide a feeling of security for the kitten. Wire carriers are easy to clean and their openness allows for air circulation in the summer, but they can be cold and drafty in the winter and provide little refuge for a frightened feline. Soft-sided carriers are lighter to carry but offer little protection if thrown about in a car accident. Wicker carriers are aesthetically pleasing, but difficult to clean.

While most carriers have a door in the side, some carriers open from the top. If a cat is difficult about going in or out of the carrier, the top-opening design makes it easier. Carriers come in different sizes so choose a size large enough to be comfortable for your cat when it reaches its adult size. Some carries come with wheels and over the shoulder straps to make transport easier. You can buy a cage cover to prevent drafts in cold weather.

Beds

Most kittens enjoy having their own bed, even something as simple as a cardboard box with an old towel on the bottom. Cut one side low enough that the kitten can enter and exit easily. If adding a foam cushion, choose one with a washable, removable cover.

Bowls

▲ Sleeping is a subject in which cats excel, and there are a wide range of cat and kitten beds available.

The kitten will need separate food plates and water bowls. Avoid plastic as it can cause a skin condition called rodent ulcers on the mouth of some cats.

Plastic also scratches, providing an ideal place for bacteria to grow. Ceramic or stainless steel is a better choice. Avoid double bowls with water on one side and food on the other. The food tends to slop into the water and vice versa. Wash and refill both food and water bowls at least once daily.

Food and Water

Abruptly changing a cat's food can lead to digestive disturbances, so initially, continue feeding the kitten the food it is accustomed to eating. Use bottled water to avoid tummy upset, gradually switching to your home tap water.

Litter Tray and Litter

The new kitten will need a shallow tray filled with the brand of cat litter to which it is used to. As the kitten grows, buy a bigger tray so the kitten always has lots of room. A covered litter tray helps contain the litter and odours, and a removable plastic liner makes changing litter easier. Self-cleaning litter trays feature an automated electro-nic cleaning arm. If you have multiple cats, allow for one more litter tray than the number of cats. Litter options include clay, scoopable, absorbent crystals and pine or paper pellets. Scoop and dispose of waste at least once daily. Change the litter completely and wash the tray weekly.

Scratching Posts and Cat Trees

Provide a carpeted or sisal scratching post to avoid damage to your furniture. A tall cat tree will give the kitten plenty opportunity to climb and exercise. Place the post in a place that is easily accessible to the cat, near a favourite spot for napping is a good

location. Sprinkle with catnip to encourage the cat to use the post. When the cat uses the post, provide positive reinforcement with petting and praise.

Grooming Tools

Grooming tools vary depending on the cat's coat. At a minimum, purchase a fine-toothed comb, brush, blunt-tipped scissors and nail clippers. Other options include a wide-toothed comb, a flea comb, hard rubber brush, grooming glove and chamois.

Collar and Leash

A collar with a tag is the easiest form of identification for your kitten. Always purchase a breakaway collar so that if the collar is caught on something, it will not injure your kitten. Most cats can also be taught to walk on a leash.

The Indoor Cat

The most important thing you can do to insure you and your cat will have a long life together is to keep your cat indoors. Studies prove that indoor cats live longer and healthier lives than outdoor cats. The indoor cat is less likely to be injured in a fight or car accident or acquire an

▶ The tools that you use to groom your cat will depend on the length and texture of its coat.

infectious disease. Responsible breeders of pedigreed cats often make keeping a kitten indoors one of their conditions of sale.

Cat Proofing Your Home

Like a child, a kitten can find dangers in its new home. You will need to cat-proof your home before introducing the kitten. Block off small spaces in which it could become stuck, cover exposed electrical outlets and close windows, etc. Kittens love to chew, especially when teething around four to five months old. Putting nasty tasting products such as Bitter Apple (a bitter-tasting liquid available at most pet stores) on objects the kitten is attracted to can discourage chewing. It is especially important to wrap electrical cords in plastic tubing to prevent the kitten from biting through and being shocked.

Dangerous When Eaten Cats have a very different physiology than humans; some things are harmless to humans, but toxic to cats. These foods include onions, green tomatoes, raw egg yolk, raw potatoes,

grapes, raisins, bones and aspirin. Chocolate, if ingested in sufficient quantities, can cause cardiac arrest. Many common plants such as philodendrons and ivy are dangerous if eaten. The traditional poinsettia at Christmas is a beautiful plant but is also toxic to cats.

Kittens are playful and curious – and will put anything in their mouths. Examine all toys for possible danger in the same way you would do for a human baby. Toys should

◀ Cats may be tempted to play with wires, so it is important to ensure electrical cords are covered in plastic tubing.

have any parts or decorations removed from them that a kitten might swallow – plastic eyes, ears, noses on a toy mouse, for instance can be pulled off in play and ingested.

Be sure to dispose of dental floss where the kitten cannot get into it. All cats eventually tip over a waste paper basket to investigate, so if it doesn't have a lid, please do not put used floss in your bathroom basket.

Other Dangers Kittens love to sleep where it is warm – including a clothes dryer, so always shut the door when the machine is not in use and always check before turning it on. If a kitten falls in a toilet, it can drown, so put down the lid. If you have a reclining chair, be aware a kitten may be asleep under it and be caught in the mechanism. Avoid leaving the cat alone with yarn, string, or toys attached to a string because the cat could accidentally swallow the string or become entangled, causing a serious emergency.

Enriching the Cat's Environment

Once your home is safe for the kitten, you will want to provide an environment that encourages your indoor cat to be active and entertained and both mentally and physically healthy.

Toys and Games Select different types of toys including soft balls, hard balls, balls with bells, catnip toys, teasers, toys with feathers, laser pointer or a racetrack. Cats are curious creatures that enjoy having places to play hide and seek. Open cardboard boxes and paper bags make safe and inexpensive toys to enrich your cat's playground. It is amusing to watch how a cat can pretend that it is hidden completely when its

▶ Curious kittens can drown if they fall into a toilet bowl, so it is best to leave the lid down.

head is in a paper bag while the rest of the body remains outside. Cut a few holes to peek through and your cat will enjoy it even more. A cardboard box with holes cut into it placed over a catnip toy or ball will allow your cat to reach through and bat at the toy.

High Up Cats like to see the world from an elevated angle. They seek high places to nap and enjoy observing the world around them. Provide window perches or indoor climbing trees for the cat to climb. For the older cat that is having troubles jumping to high places, you can construct a series of shelves with sturdy boxes to allow the cat to climb by jumping from box to box.

Treats Treat balls are also available that dispense treats slowly as the toy is played with. The same can be done for your cat's food. They can be placed in various locations of the house so your cat will have to search for its food. Some cats enjoy drinking from a running water tap because the water is fresher. Consider adding a drinking water fountain for cats to keep the water moving continuously.

Playtime Cats like to chase, pounce and hunt. You can attach feathers or rolled up pieces of cardboard to a wire or stuffed toys strings with a wand to create a toy that bounces around. These toys encourage your cat to jump and 'hunt' like a real lion. You can make time to play with your cat, even if it is just for a few minutes of the day.

▶ Cats enjoy playing with a range of toys, including chew toys, balls, catnip, string and cardboard boxes.

Room with a View Rare is the cat that does not appreciate a room with a view. The window should be closed or protected well enough so the cat cannot escape. Add a shelf so the cat can sit and see out comfortably. This gives the cat the opportunity to observe the world outside and sniff some fresh air. Many cats will stay by a window with a good view for hours, especially if there are squirrels or birds outside.

Children Involve children when thinking of ways to keep your cat active. Children can play with the cat using toys, such as throwing ping-pong balls or playing with a toy attached to a string. Under adult supervision, a laser pointer beam could be used for cats to chase. For very young children, the key to safe play with the kitten is adult supervision.

Outdoor Times Finally, cats can be trained to use a leash when outdoors with their owner. Although most cats do not walk down the street alongside their owners like dogs do, cats can be accustomed to having a leash on and knowing their limits. A harness attached to a leash is most commonly used. Being on a leash prevents the cat from getting lost or hit by a car while allowing it to enjoy the sights, sounds and smells of the great outdoors under your supervision. Remember that it is a good idea to have a collar with ID tags on when your cat is outdoors in the event that it escapes from the harness. Never leave a cat tied even for a few minutes because the leash could get caught somewhere and strangle the cat or the cat may escape.

The Outdoor Cat

Some cats live an indoor/ outdoor life, spending part of the day indoors, and part outdoors. One advantage of allowing your cat outdoors is a reduction in litter tray chores. You will, however, need to respond to the cats every meow at the door to be let out. And there is always the possibility of complaints from neighbours who do not appreciate the cat doing its duty in their flowerbeds.

The outdoor cat may develop a more independent personality as its wild instincts surface, bonding more with the outdoor environment than with its human family. The greatest drawback of allowing your cat outdoors is the risk to its life and health.

The Dangers Faced By the Outdoor Cat

While a cat may enjoy the stimulus of the great outdoors, it is also faced with a long list of perils. The outdoor cat is subject to injury or death by vehicles, intentional or accidental poisoning, fighting with other cats, exposure to parasites or infectious diseases from other cats, injury or death by dogs or predators and becoming lost. It may be picked up by animal control or be the cause of complaints from neighbours.

Identification

The outdoor cat should have some form of identification in case it becomes lost or injured. A breakaway collar with a

◀ Outdoor cats are prone to many health risks, including the
possibility of being run over.*

tag including your name, address and phone number is a must. A second tag with your vet's information is an added bonus. Because a cat can lose its collar, it is important that it also be microchipped. In case the cat does go missing, be sure to have a good, clear photograph to help others recognize your cat.

Cat Flap

A cat flap is a hinged flap set into a door, wall or window to allow a cat to enter and exit a house at will, freeing their human from the need to open the door, while offering a degree of protection against wind and rain entering the dwelling. Cat flaps are popular in some countries, particularly the United Kingdom where it is believed that about 90 per cent of cats have access to the outdoors. The downside of the cat flap is that it can allow other animals into the house and cats can also bring mice and birds into the dwelling through the flaps.

Building an Outdoor Enclosure

If you were going to allow your cat outdoors, the ideal solution would be to have a cat-proof back yard. There are special fencing systems available that can be added to existing fences to make them more difficult for a cat to climb. Another option is to build an outdoor enclosure. It can be free standing or attached to the home and allow your cat the best of both worlds – a feeling of freedom of the outdoors, while protected from the danger of the outdoors.

◀ A cat flap offers a great deal of freedom, but can also allow unwanted visitors into your home.

On your Travels

Home Alone

If fed a diet of dry cat food, most cats can be left home alone for two days. A full bowl of dry food or a feeding tower will be more than adequate. A large bowl of water, a water bottle or a running tap will provide water. You could ask a helpful neighbour to look in once a day. Cats are sometimes anxious and distressed when left alone for longer periods of time. Some cats are upset at the change in routine, so leave the television on. Two cats will keep one another company, though they may also get into more mischief.

The Pet Sitter

Some cat owners in urban areas prefer to have a cat sitter visit the home daily, or in some cases live in if they are going to be gone for an extended time. Start with a recommendation from a friend, neighbour, vet or check the telephone directory under 'Pet Sitting Services.' Have the prospective pet sitter visit your home to meet your cat before actually hiring them. Watch how the sitter interacts with your pet – does your cat seem comfortable with the person? If the visit goes well, hire the sitter while you go on a weekend away, before leaving for longer periods.

The Boarding Cattery

While most cats are happier remaining in their own home, as long as they have a social personality, they can also be fine in a quality boarding facility set up specifically for cats. Ask to see the cattery well before time. All

◄ A cat can be left alone for a day or two if provided with water and a plentiful supply of dry food.

boarding facilities are not created equal. The best cat facilities offer an indoor-outdoor area, allow you to bring your cat's bed, toys and favourite food and are out of sight and sound of barking dogs.

Travel by Car

Contrary to popular opinion, many cats make good car travellers. The key is to take them on enjoyable rides while they are young so they become comfortable with car travel. Take the kitten on frequent short trips; a trip to the supermarket and back. The kitten will soon take car rides for granted – just part of a cat's normal routine.

Travel by Aeroplane

Many airlines permit you to travel with your cat in the cabin if the carrier is small enough to fit under the seat in front of you. You will be required to purchase a pet ticket. Alternatively, the cat can fly in cargo, in a special area reserved for live animals. It must be in an airline-approved carrier. Every airline has different requirements and restrictions regarding flying with a pet. Contact the specific airline you plan on flying with to obtain their specifications. You will be required to show proof of current vaccinations and obtain a health certificate within ten days of travel. Exhibitors fly with show cats often and most cats are good flyers.

Use of Tranquillizers

It is not usually recommended to tranquillize a cat for travel. Reactions to tranquillizers vary, and it can actually make them more agitated.

▶ A boarding cattery can be an option for full-time pet care while you are away on holiday.

Caring for your
Cat

Care of your New Kitten

You've chosen your kitten. Everyone is excited! The day has arrived to bring the new family member home. The best time to welcome your kitten to its new home is on a weekend or when you will have several days off work to take the time to help settle it into its new surroundings. Here is some advice on getting the kitten home safely, what to do in the first 24 hours and thereafter.

Bringing Kitty Home

A suitable cat carrier is essential to the safe transport of your kitten. As much as you may prefer to snuggle the cat in your lap on the trip home in the car, a cat should always travel in the safety of a carrier. If you hold the kitten in your arms in the car and it is startled by a honking horn or noisy traffic, it may struggle loose, scratching or biting. Once loose, it could cause an accident by scrambling under the brake pedal or distracting the driver. Be safe, not sorry.

Place a small blanket or towel in the bottom of the carrier for the kitten to snuggle on. The stress of travelling can lead to an 'accident', so bring paper towels and replacement bedding, just in case.

▶ When a kitten is first brought home, it is best to confine it to one room, preferably a bedroom.

The First 24 Hours

The first 24 hours with your new kitten are the most important time. The kitten may feel lonely, missing its littermates or frightened and insecure in its unfamiliar new environment. Begin by confining it to one room, usually a bedroom, preferably of an adult family member. The kitten's most immediate needs are to learn where its food, water and litter tray is in its new home. Make sure they are within sight.

Bring the kitten into the room in its carrier and open the door. An extroverted kitten may come bounding out ready to explore its new environment. The shy kitten may feel intimidated and not come out immediately. The cave-like carrier is comforting. Don't force the kitten. Let it take its time while encouraging it to come out. Sit on the floor. It is less intimidating. Speak in soft, soothing tones. Use a small teaser to see if you can encourage the kitten to play, but also allow the kitten time to investigate its surroundings. Once the kitten seems comfortable in its new room, offer it food or a treat. Introduce it to the litter tray.

Everyone in the family will want to pet and hold it, especially children. It is easy for the kitten to feel overwhelmed. Do not introduce it to too many family members at one time. Warn small children to sit quietly and let the kitten come to them rather than allowing them to chase the kitten. They need to understand the kitten is not a toy and must be given its own space.

At bedtime, place the kitten in its bed. Sometimes a kitten will feel safer in the carrier, so leave its on the floor with the door open. Do not allow the kitten to sleep on your bed unless that is something you are going to permit it all the time.

Once the kitten feels secure in 'its room', open the door and let it explore the rest of the home at its own pace. If you have another cat or dog, confine it so the kitten has a chance to investigate the home without having to encounter another animal. As the cat gains more confidence, the time will come to introduce the kitten to other family pets.

Veterinary Exam

Within 24–72 hours of bringing your new kitten home, take it to your veterinarian for a complete and thorough checkup. Your veterinarian will be able to confirm the kitten is in good health, free of parasites or hidden health problems. If bought from a breeder, a vet check is often part of their contract and validates the purchase.

This is the time to have the kitten microchipped. A small electronic chip is inserted just under the skin between the shoulder blades. A hand-held scanner can read the number that is registered in your name. It allows your kitten to be identified should it ever be lost or stolen. If your kitten has not seen a veterinarian previously, this is also the time it should receive its initial vaccinations.

Carrying the Kitten

Handle the kitten gently. Rough or sudden movements may startle it. To carry it, slip the palm of one hand under its tummy and support its rear end with your other hand.

▶ Kittens should be taken to the vet for a general checkup within three days of arriving at your home.

Introduction to Another Cat or Dog

Always supervise the introduction of the kitten with other family pets. Begin by allowing the kitten and resident pet to sniff one another underneath the door. They may even play a game of footsie. This allows them to become accustomed to one another's scent. An adult cat may feel territorial and resent the kitten initially. Don't be surprised if there is some initial growling or hissing. This is not unusual. You can use a pet gate to separate a dog from the kitten. Or put the kitten in a cage, allowing the dog to approach and investigate, but preventing a physical confrontation. Act as a chaperone until you are confident the animals will get along together. Often, they will end up the best of friends within a few days.

Playtime

The new kitten will needs lots of play activities. This is an excellent time for bonding. You are taking the place of its siblings. The kitten will want to chase and play with your fingers and hand, perhaps your feet

and ankles. If the kitten becomes too rough or aggressive, say no and blow softly in its face.

Personality Test

There are a few simple tests you can perform to gain insight into your kitten's personality:

▶ Introductions between a new kitten and a resident cat or dog should be conducted with care.

Testing for Socialization

Observe your kitten. A well-socialized kitten will watch you, follow you, play with your feet and make eye contact. A poorly socialized kitten may hide from you or run away when you approach. If your kitten acts afraid of you, you will need to begin the socialization process over again. Spend lots of time playing with the kitten, hand feeding it, gaining its trust.

The Toy Test

Roll a small ball in front of the kitten and see whether it chases it, or ignores it to test how well it reacts to things in its environment.

Testing For Dominance

Roll the kitten on to its back and gently stroke its tummy. If the kitten permits and enjoys the massage, it has learned to accept parental authority. If it struggles and resists, it is trying to be dominant.

The Noise Test

Stand a little distance behind your kitten. When it is not looking, clap your hands loudly three times. If the kitten turns to you and comes to investigate, it is confident. If it runs away, it has not been brought up to accept new noises and sensations.

Feeding

Good nutrition is the foundation of raising a healthy cat. Cats are carnivores; however, an all-meat diet is not balanced. In the wild, when a cat captures a mouse, it consumes everything that is edible – flesh, organs, bones and entrails. Because the mouse is herbivorous (plant-eater), when the cat eats the stomach and intestines that contain seeds and plants it receives the trace elements and vitamins needed for a nutritionally balanced diet.

Commercial cat foods are specially formulated to provide the cat's complete nutrition. The foods are standardized, convenient and less expensive than preparing home-made diets. The main advantage of feeding a commercial food is the assurance that the cat is eating a balanced diet that includes all the elements necessary for proper growth and development.

An adult cat requires about 50 calories per 450 g (1 lb) of weight per day. A very active feline may need a bit more; a less active cat requires a bit less. Most adult cats seem to thrive on either self feeding or being fed two meals a day. A cat's general appearance is a good indicator of whether its diet is satisfactory. A well-fed cat carries good weight, has a shiny coat, bright eyes and appears happy and content. Signs of poor nutrition include low body weight, dry coat, flakey skin, dull eyes, bad breath and offensive smelling stools.

Changing Foods

It is best to feed the new kitten the food it has been eating. If the kitten is purchased from a breeder, ask for their feeding recommend-ations and schedule. Once the kitten is settled in its new home, you may

investigate other feeding options. A new food may initially upset the kitten's digestive system so any change should be introduced in stages. Mix the new food in with the old in steadily increasing proportions over the course of a week. A slow transition avoids the risk of the kitten developing diarrhoea. The best food in the world is no good if your cat will not eat it, so palatability is a critical component in choosing any food.

Dry, Canned or Semi-Moist?

With the wide selection of commercial cat foods available on the market today, it can be a challenge selecting the type and brand that best suits your cat's nutritional needs. Cat food comes in three basic types; dry kibble, canned food, or semi-moist foods in pouches.

Dry foods are relatively inexpensive, convenient and have the advantage of remaining fresh in the bowl all day, allowing the cat to feed free. This is especially handy for kittens that eat multiple meals in small servings throughout the day. Dry foods should be stored in a cool, dry place, either in the closed original bag or a container with an airtight lid to keep it fresh. There is some evidence that crunching on hard kibbles helps reduce tartar build up. Dry foods usually contain 8 to 10 per cent water compared to 80 per cent water in canned food, so cats fed dry food often drink more water.

◄ There are many different types of dry food on the market; they stay fresh and are good for your cat's teeth.

► Moist food does not last once served, so you should only give your cat an amount that it can eat.

Canned food and semi-moist foods may be tastier than dry food but will spoil if not eaten immediately. Care should be taken to offer only as much food as the cat will finish in a single meal. Canned food should be refrigerated once opened and any leftover wet food should be discarded after each meal.

Protein Content

Cats are obligate carnivores, which mean they need to eat a food with high protein content from meat, poultry or fish. The breeding cat's diet should be 30–40 per cent protein, while neutered cats need about 25 per cent. Pet food labels list their ingredients on the label. Look for the first ingredient to be a species-specific protein such as chicken, beef or fish. Do not be misled by the phrase 'meat by-products'. By-products refer to heads, feet, feathers, entrails, etc, and are not a high-quality protein source.

Premium or Economy

Because a food is expensive does not mean it is necessarily better for your cat. Many mid-priced foods have good nutritional profiles. Some economy brands of cat food, however, are made from inexpensive ingredients not fit for human consumption and not easily digested. If a food is difficult to digest, you may have to feed more of it for your cat to receive the same nutritional value as feeding less of a higher quality food.

◄ Different breeds have different nutritional requirements, and so there is a range of specially formulated foods.

The Right Diet for Your Cat

Life Stage Diets

Choose a food that is made to meet the specific nutritional require-ments for the stage of life of your cat. Kittens have higher nutritional demands needed to develop and grow. As a cat enters its golden years, it can suffer from age-related problems including a weaker immune system, less efficient digestive system, decreasing senses of smell and taste, arthritis and urinary problems. Senior cats may benefit from a diet lower in phosphorus and with a moderate level of fibre to help prevent constipation and cat foods for older cats are often formulated stimulate the senior cat's appetite.

Lifestyle Diets

Cats that go outdoors may need a food higher in protein and calories than cats living exclusively indoors. Some studies suggest as many as one out of four pet cats are overweight. Commercial foods are available with reduced fat content and high protein levels that help the obese feline lose weight without losing muscle mass.

Special Diets

There are different cat foods specifically for felines with food allergies, sensitive tummies, heart or urinary problems, dental disease and coat or skin problems. Hairballs can cause vomiting and diarrhoea but specially formulated food helps to improve digestive and transit through the intestines. Foods are available to meet the different nutritional needs of specific breeds of cats including Persians, Maine Coons and Siamese. There are even cat foods that claim to reduce the amount of stool and its odour.

▶ Some cats are prone to putting on weight, but there are many types of diet cat food available.

Home-made Diets

Some cat owners believe in home-made or raw meat diets. Care must be used if preparing home-made meals for your cat. While you can easily control the quality of ingredients, you can never be entirely sure of its nutritional balance. Home-prepared food is usually more expensive than commercial, perishable and time consuming to prepare.

Supplements, Treats and Table Scraps

If you are feeding a good-quality food, it is not necessary to add a supplement. An occasional treat from your plate shouldn't hurt, as long as it does not take the place of a cat's normal food. Several human foods are very toxic or dangerous to cats. Never feed pork, chocolate, onions, green tomatoes, raw egg yolk, raw potatoes, grapes, raisins, bones or dog food to your cat, just to name a few.

Water

Your cat should always have access to fresh water. Water bowls should be cleaned and refilled daily. Contrary to popular opinion, cow's milk is not good for cats. Not only is it difficult for a cat to digest, it often causes diarrhoea.

▶ Cats may be given milk occasionally as a treat, providing they do not show signs of lactose intolerance.

Training

When it comes to behaviour, some cats are naturally 'purrfect' (or almost), while others have a little more tiger in them. Whether your cat bites your hand, plays in the middle of the night or climbs your leg while you prepare dinner, such antics require behaviour modification. There are various techniques that can be used to encourage more acceptable behaviour in your cat. You can even take it further and train them to perform simple 'tricks' and agility manoeuvres.

Positive Reinforcement

Cats are not dogs. The training techniques that work well with our canine friends are not particularly effective with the feline psyche. Cats work best when rewarded with treats, so discover a food that your cat responds to as a reward. It may be a cat treat, a sliver of cooked meat or a tiny taste of chicken baby food. Of course, do not ruin their properly balanced diet. Once your cat performs the task requested, reward it with both a treat and praise.

◄ When attempting to train your cat, edible rewards can be one of the most effective methods.

You should never hit your cat as punishment, but there are other forms of discipline that are effective. A spritz of water from a spray bottle or water pistol will often discourage unwelcome behaviour. The key is to not let the cat realize the spray came from you if possible. In closer quarters, blowing in the cat's face can be an effective deterrent. The puff of air can be varied in strength, number and duration to best suit the cat and the behaviour. Loud clapping, rattling cans, imitating a cat's hiss or a blast from an air horn are also effective deterrents with some felines.

Common Unacceptable Behaviours

Biting

Unwarranted biting is not acceptable from your cat under any circumstances. If it happens, pinch the cat's tongue and hold on for a few seconds.

Jumping up on worktops

Jumping on kitchen surfaces can be very dangerous – your cat could walk on a hot cooker top. If your cat jumps up when you are present, keep a spray bottle handy and spritz the cat as it is in mid-leap. If it jumps up only when it thinks you are not looking, watch unobserved and just as it is thinking of jumping up, blow a whistle.

◄ Jumping on to worktops can be dangerous, so it is important to train your cat not to do this.

Digging In The House Plants

A cat may be tempted to use the dirt in a plant pot as a litter tray. Simply fill the top of the container with small stones.

Scratching on Furniture

The best thing you can do for your furniture is to train your kitten to use a scratching post. Place several scratching posts conveniently around the house. Praise the cat when it uses them. If a kitten starts to scratch on furniture, say 'No' loudly and take it to the scratching post.

If a cat starts to claw furniture, spritz it with water, or startle it by tossing a newspaper or car keys toward it. If you cover a favourite scratching spot with aluminum foil or two-sided sticky tape, a cat will often be discouraged. A mild menthol, vinegar or citrus scent also repels some cats. Once your cat realizes that these places are not fun to scratch it will prefer the scratching post.

Inappropriate Urination

If your cat is urinating or defecating outside the litter tray, a veterinary checkup is necessary to eliminate a possible medical reason. If there is no health problem, confine the cat to a small room with a cat bed at one end and a litter tray at the other. Praise your cat for using the litter tray. If you catch your cat in the act of urinating or defecating outside of the tray (or even starting the digging motion), startle it by tossing a drinks can with a few coins inside of it towards the cat (but not at it) to make it stop. You could also use a whistle or water pistol.

Clean the area where the cat has urinated inappropriately then spray it with cologne or place a plastic carpet runner upside down with the spikes pointing up to discourage the cat from returning to the spot. Double sided tape, pet repellents or a scat mat are other options.

Midnight Crazies

Some cats come to life at night. The cat stampedes through the house, playing with toys and often jumping on beds hoping the human occupants will 'come out and play'. Keep it confined to one room at night, and try to change its activity patterns by playing more with it during the day and especially before bedtime so it it's more likely to be tired.

Chewing

Cats chew on inappropriate objects such as clothing, electrical cords, or papers. Make the objects taste unpleasant by spraying them with vinegar, hot-pepper sauce or Bitter Apple.

Teaching Your Cat Tricks

Cats are not only capable of learning simple commands; they enjoy the interaction with their 'person' and look forward to being a 'star'. So as not to confuse them, work with one command at a time. Be consistent and patient, letting your cat work at its own speed. Reward the cat enthusiastically at the first sign of understanding.

Come With food treat in hand, and preferably when your cat is hungry, call 'come'. As it comes to investigate, praise it and give it the treat. The cat will quickly learn to associate the food with the

▶ To ensure your cat does not get a nasty shock, cover all electrical wire with plastic tubing.

◀ You can teach your cat to sit up by dangling treats above it while giving the command.

command. Never call a cat to punish him or to do something to it that it may not enjoy – like a bath or medications – as the association will change into a negative one.

Shake a Paw With your cat sitting in front of you, touch his paw and say 'shake.' As soon as it lifts the paw, shake it and give him a treat and praise.

Sit-Up With your cat in a sitting position, hold a treat over its head and say 'sit-up.' Do not give it the reward if it stands or grabs at the treat, but repeat the command and try again. When it sits up, give it the treat immediately.

Playing Fetch To teach fetch, it helps if your cat has a bit of an oral fixation. It should like carrying things around in its mouth. If you notice a kitten walking around with a toy in its mouth give it lots of praise. The more excited your cat is about the fetch object, the more likely it will 'grab' it and carry it. Throw the toy and command 'Fetch'. Unlike in teaching other tricks, a food reward is less effective in encouraging a cat to fetch. The reward is that the object is thrown again. The cat must enjoy the game of fetch or else it will simply chase the ball without returning it to you.

Agility Training and Competition

A new competition offered at some cat shows is called cat agility. Similar to dog agility, a cat and its handler negotiate an obstacle course designed to demonstrate the cat's athletic ability, speed, coordination and the quality of the animal's training relationship with its owner. The event is timed with points taken off for obstacles missed or incomplete. Typical obstacles include ramps, platforms, tunnels, jumps, hoop, weave poles and steps. The handler uses a long teaser or wand to direct and encourage the cat to go over, through or around the obstacles. The course is completely fenced so a cat cannot go astray.

▶ In extreme cases, cat agility courses can include obstacles such as flaming hoops.

Grooming

The term 'grooming' as used here, implies all the things that can or should be done by you in order to maintain your cat's appearance – including keeping the nails at bay, combing and brushing the coat, bathing, cleaning the ears and even brushing their teeth. Although cats are very good at grooming and cleaning themselves, they need a helping hand from their owners to remain in peak condition.

Grooming is important not just for aesthetic reasons but also for health ones – not least because it allows you to check for any physical changes while carrying out the grooming process.

Nail Clipping

Begin clipping the kitten's nails early and it will become used to the procedure. Trim once every week or two. Select a scissor-style cat nail clipper with two cutting edges, or cuticle trimmers on human toenail clippers. Place the cat on a table or your lap. Hold the cat's paw and extend the retracted claw by pressing the toe between your thumb and forefinger. If the nail is white, you will see the 'quick', the blood vessel that runs through the centre. Trim the nail to within 2 mm ($\frac{1}{16}$ in) of the quick in one quick motion. If you accidentally cut into the quick and it bleeds use a blood stop powder or a septic pencil to stop the bleeding.

▶ If you clip your kitten's nails from an early age, it will grow accustomed to the process.

Combing

Regular combing helps to remove the dead hair that can result in hairballs. A comb penetrates the coat better than a brush. Begin at the head working towards the tail, and down from the back and work to the tummy. Comb in the direction of the hair and then against it to gently remove dead hair. Lift the chin and comb the chest. Roll the cat on its back in your lap and comb the underside. Take special care when working around the sensitive genital area.

A weekly session with a small, close-toothed comb is usually sufficient for a shorthaired cat. After combing, repeat with a hard rubber brush and if you like, finish off by rubbing with a chamois or silk cloth.

Longhaired cats, especially Persians, require daily grooming with a wide-toothed comb. Repeat with a fine-toothed comb. Pay special attention to the rear britches, checking for dried faeces that may be stuck on the hair (affectionately called 'clingons'). Knots can be gently teased out while mats are a job for a professional groomer. During the spring and summer when the cat is shedding, comb more frequently.

Bathing

All cats can learn to accept being bathed. Bathing washes away loose hair, reducing shed on the furniture and removes excess oil, keeping the cat clean. A cat can be bathed as often as you like as long as you use mild shampoo. Show Persians are often bathed twice a week.

A convenient place to bathe the cat is the kitchen sink, especially if it has a spray attachment. Place a rubber mat in the bottom to stop the cat from slipping. Place the

cat in an empty sink, wet the coat using the spray then fill the sink with water halfway. Dilute the shampoo and work through the coat from head to tail, from back to belly. Finish with a conditioner and rise thoroughly.

Avoid getting water in the eyes or ears. Some cats, particularly flat-faced cats such as Persians, accumulate tears under the eyes and in the creases that run on either side of the nose. A face cloth damped with warm water is sufficient to clean the face, especially the build up of secretions around the eyes. Dry nasal secretions in the corner of their nostrils can be removed with a cotton pad or tissue.

Squeeze as much water out of the coat as possible with your hands. Wrap the cat in a towel to absorb more moisture. Finish drying the hair with a hairdryer. Professional pet dryers are available that dry faster.

Cleaning the Ears

Use a cotton swab or make-up pad moistened with warm water or mineral oil to clean the inside of the external ear. Never use alcohol as it is too drying. Do not probe down into the ear as you may cause injury. If there is a particularly obvious and unpleasant looking discharge, consult your vet.

Brushing Your Cat's Teeth

Tuna-flavoured toothpaste and a finger brush can be used to brush your cat's teeth and help prevent tartar build up.

◄ Brushing your cat's teeth can help to prevent tartar build-up; tuna-flavoured toothpaste is available.

► A cat's ears can be cleaned by gently folding them back and wiping with a moistened pad or cotton bud.

Health

You've done your homework, found an adorable new kitten, 'cat proofed' your home and chosen an appropriate carrier, bed, food and toys. Now you look forward with excitement to the joy the new feline will bring to your life. In exchange, you will need to provide love and attention, good nutrition and medical care including regular checkups at your vet's. There are also a certain amount of feline ailments that it is worth knowing a little about in order to be alert to changes in your cat's health.

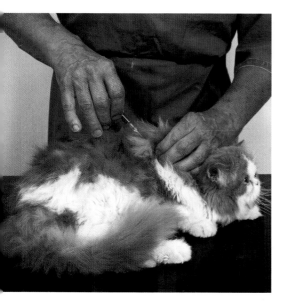

Routine Health Care

Checkups

Within 24–72 hours of bringing the new kitten home, it is time for its first visit to the vet. This will give your vet the opportunity to gather basic information regarding the kitten's health and begin its medical record. The vet will evaluate the kitten's general body condition, take its temperature, listen to the heart and lungs, check the eyes and look in the ears and mouth. A thorough physical examination will include checking for parasites.

◄ Boosters to your cat's initial course of vaccinations are usually recommended every year.

Worming Bring a fresh bowel movement to test for internal parasites. If necessary, the kitten will be wormed.

Vaccinations Bring information you have been given regarding vaccinations the kitten has already received. Most vets recommend that kittens be vaccinated against several common infectious diseases. A single vaccine called FVRCP protects against a combination of diseases; Feline viral rhinotracheitis (FVR), Feline calicivirus (C), and Feline panleukopenia (P). The first inoculation is usually given at eight weeks with a booster at 12 weeks. A rabies inoculation is given at 16 weeks. Boosters are recommended annually. Depending on individual risks, vaccinations against feline leukaemia (FeLV) and chlamydia are an option.

Spaying and Neutering

A female cat should be spayed, and a male neutered if they are not to be used for breeding. The traditional age for spaying and neutering was once six months, but with improvements in anesthesia, many vets now offer early procedures, sometimes as young as seven weeks of age as long as the kitten weighs a minimum of 1 kg (2 lb). This practice is particularly common in animal shelters.

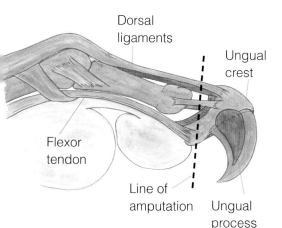

Dorsal ligaments

Ungual crest

Flexor tendon

Line of amputation

Ungual process

De-clawing and Tendonectomy

Cats in the wild use their claws to climb, hunt and mark their territory. This instinctive behaviour can lead to destruction of furniture if the indoor cat is not trained to use a scratching post. If a cat has not been taught to

◄ De-clawing a cat. De-clawing is controversial and illegal in some countries.

► Your cat should be spayed or neutered if you are not planning to breed from it, to prevent unwanted kittens.

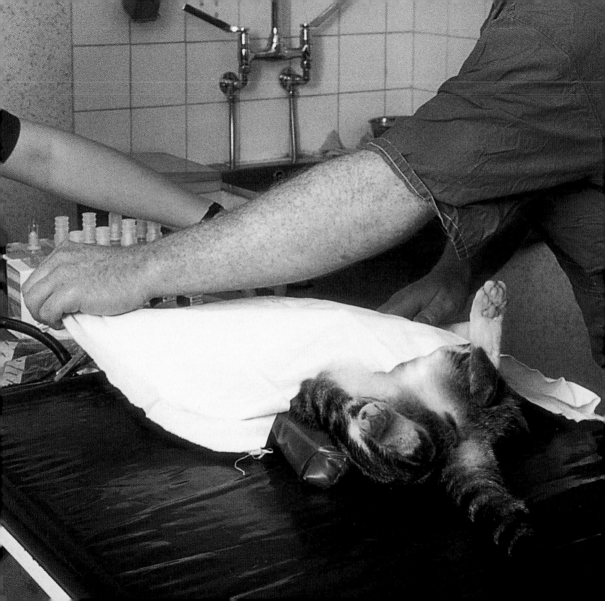

use a scratching post, some owners consider having the cat de-clawed, a controversial elective procedure. Illegal in some countries including Britain (except for medical reasons), de-clawing is the surgical removal of the claw by amputating the last digit of the toe. Most breeders of pedigreed cats include a clause in their kitten contract stating the cat must not be de-clawed. Many vets refuse to perform the surgery except as a last resort in cases of extreme behavioural problems.

A tendonectomy is the surgical removal of part of the flexor tendons. The claws are left in place, but with the flexor tendon severed the cat cannot extend the claws, preventing use of the claw to scratch. While less invasive than de-clawing, a tendonectomy also fundamentally alters the function of the cat's foot and nails.

'Soft Paws' is a vinyl nail cap that fits over the claw and can be effective if it remains in place. But a little effort training the young kitten to use a scratching post is well worth it for the cat's mental and physical wellbeing.

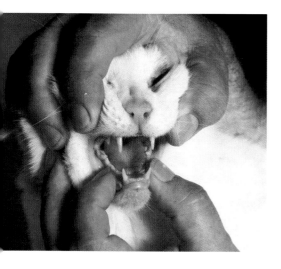

Dental Care

Over time, tartar deposits build up on the teeth causing inflammation of the gums, bad breath and, in extreme cases, can lead to teeth falling out. Tarter is not difficult to remove, provided it has not been permitted to become too thick. Heavy deposits of tarter require special dental tools. An improper diet, especially one deficient in calcium and phosphorus, can lead to poor tooth health.

◄ It is important to keep your cat's teeth and gums healthy as well as tartar-free.

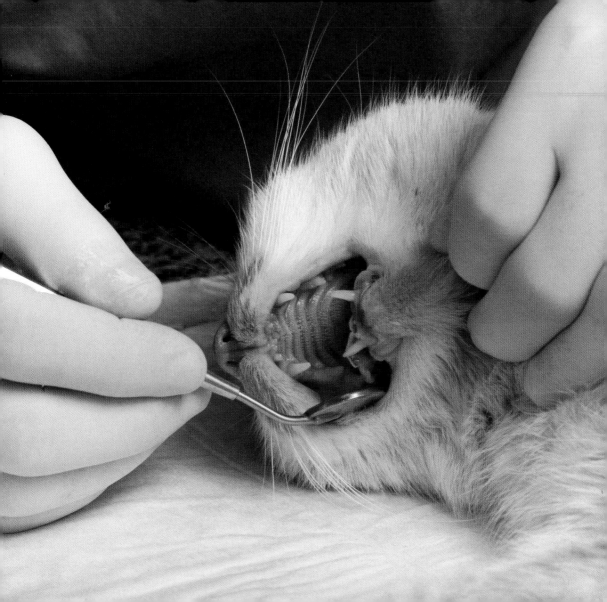

Signs of Illness

The Healthy Cat

A cat in good health appears sleek and well muscled, but not fat. The coat is glossy and soft to the touch, with no excessive shedding except in the spring. The skin is free of sores, eczema or fleas. Bowel movements are regular and well formed, with little odour and at least one per day as an adult. The normal rectal temperature is 101–102 °F. The mouth should be free of sores, the gums pink with no sign of gingivitis and little or no breath odour. Eyes should be bright without redness or discharge. The nose and ears are clean and free of discharge although a healthy cat may occasionally cough or sneeze. The cat has a healthy appetite, appears alert, curious, active, playful and purrs contentedly when petted.

Indications of Illness

Most felines are stoic, often hiding any symptoms of illness. This is a natural instinct in the wild to avoid being perceived as vulnerable by predators. Because a cat cannot tell us if it is not feeling well, the responsibility falls to the owner to be observant, sensitive to signs that something may be wrong. To complicate matters, often the difference between a minor health problem and something seriously wrong is only a matter of degree. Kittens and elderly cats are more vulnerable. When in doubt, call your vet. Signs of illness requiring veterinary attention include:

- ▶ Any significant behavioural change
- ▶ Not eating or drinking for more than 24 hours
- ▶ Drinking excessively or sitting with the head hanging over the water bowl
- ▶ Listlessness or sleeping more than usual

> ▶ If your cat seems to sleep excessively, it could be an indication that it is need of veterinary attention.

- Vomiting repeatedly in one day, vomiting repeatedly over several days or if vomiting is accompanied by fatigue, listlessness, diarrhoea or blood. Cats may vomit for a variety of harmless reasons but prolonged vomiting is indicative of serious trouble
- Excessive shedding, bare spots and sores on the skin or a dull, dry and lifeless coat
- Constipation, diarrhoea, bloody stools or difficult bowel movements
- Frequent urination, straining while urinating, dark or blood-tinged urine or inability to urinate. Going in and out of the litter tray repeatedly, crying while urinating or producing little or no urine are all signs of an infection or a blocked bladder
- Loss of control of bowels or bladder
- Fever
- Excessive sneezing or coughing
- Pawing or scratching at the head or ears
- Change in pupil dilation
- Eye(s) squinted shut for more than four hours
- Heavy, thick or discoloured mucus from eyes and nose
- The third eyelid is visible (though in some cats, a portion of the third eyelid is visible at all times and it is not always a sign of illness)
- Blood from mouth, eyes, ears, anus, penis or vulva
- Pale gums or ears
- Swellings or abscesses on the face, legs, or tail
- Wounds, cuts or contusions
- New lumps or swellings anywhere on the body, particularly ones that are growing
- Any injury that has a bad odour
- Limping or holding up a leg
- Sudden weight loss or gain

▶ Checking the condition of your cat's mouth and gums can help to ascertain its state of health.

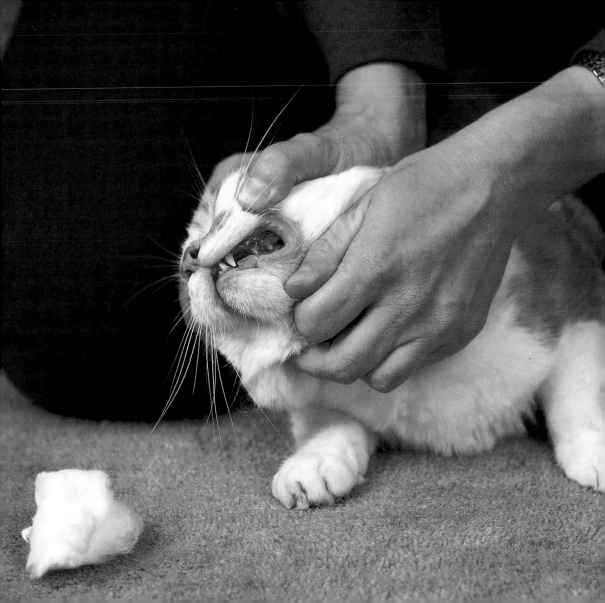

▷ Distended stomach

▷ Obvious pain or sensitivity to being touched or held

▷ Disorientation or loss of motor skills

▷ Difficulty or laboured breathing

▷ Limping or refusal to walk

Feline Ailments

External Parasites

External parasites are found feeding on the skin and hair of the cat and are more common in cats that go outdoors.

Ear mites are microscopic parasites that live in the ear canal, feeding on fluid in the tissue. Symptoms include black, waxy discharge, shaking the head, holding the head or ear at an odd angle or scratching the ear.

Fleas are tiny insects that feed on blood and create mild to severe discomfort. If swallowed, they can transmit tapeworms. Symptoms include itching, dark,

▼ A deer tick feeds on a cat; ticks should never be pulled out, as the head may remain under the skin.

◀ The dark flecks in this cat's coat are evidence that there are fleas present.

comma-shaped flecks in your cat's fur or skin, or sleep and play areas. Some cats develop an allergic dermatitis to fleabites.

Fur mites, sometimes called walking dandruff, infest the skin causing itching and flaking and can infect people.

Ticks are picked up almost exclusively outdoors, preferring to attach themselves around the neck and ears, causing an inflammatory reaction where they attach. Never pull on a tick to remove it as you risk leaving the head's tick under the skin, which can cause a painful reaction.

Internal Parasites

Kittens are far more susceptible to internal parasites than adult cats. The major internal parasites are divided into two categories; 'worms' and microscopic protozoa.

Roundworms These spaghetti-like worms lodge in the kitten's small intestine, form balls and can cause intestinal obstructions. They can be detected by the presence of microscopic eggs in the kitten's faeces. Symptoms include vomiting, diarrhoea and a distended stomach.

Tapeworms are common intestinal parasites acquired when a cat ingests an infected flea or outdoor cats eat rabbits, mice or other rodents. Tapeworms are segmented worms that attach to the intestinal wall and cause bloating, diarrhoea and sometimes damage to the coat. They can be detected by the presence of white segment like grains of rice in the stool.

Hookworm Though these are uncommon, symptoms include weakness, anaemia and diarrhoea.

▶ Kittens are particularly susceptible to numerous internal parasites.

Heartworm is less commonly seen in cats than dogs but can be fatal. Testing and preventive medications are recommended for cats at high risk.

Giardia are microscopic protozoa that attach to the mucous membrane of the small intestine causing incomplete digestion, diarrhoea and gradual loss of weight.

Coccidia are parasites of the digestive system contracted from infected mice or birds or the faeces of infected cats. Symptoms include diarrhoea, weight loss, and listlessness, especially in kittens.

Toxoplasmosis is a serious disease transmitted by eating contaminated food or by contact with infected nasal discharge, saliva and faeces of carrier animals. Young cats are most susceptible. Symptoms include fever, loss of appetite, cough, jaundice, emaciation, laboured breathing and nervous system disturbances. Most infected cats develop a natural immunity. If transmitted to a pregnant woman, Toxoplasmosis can cause miscarriage or birth defects. For this reason, pregnant women should avoid cleaning litter trays, or at least wear protective gloves.

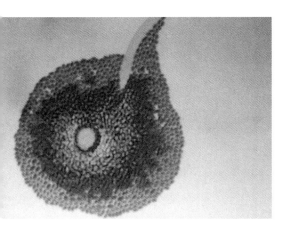

Skin Problems

Ringworm is a fungal infection characterized by small, round, crusty, hairless spots, especially around neck and ears. It is resistant, widely spread and contagious to most animals including humans. Treatment is lengthy and both animals and their environment need to be treated.

◄ Ringworm is a highly contagious fungal infection and can spread from cats to their owners.

▶ Pregnant women should avoid cleaning litter trays.

Abscesses are small swellings on the skin caused by an accumulation of blood, lymph or fluids resulting from an animal bite, scratch, insect sting or a vaccination site reaction. Symptoms include swelling, pain or sensitivity to touch, loss of appetite, irritability and fever. Ice packs or cold cloths may reduce the swelling but surgical drainage is often necessary.

Feline Acne looks like dirt on the chin and is the result of small oily black plugs in the chin, like blackheads, that may develop into red, itchy bumps, which may in turn become infected. Treatment varies, but may include daily cleaning with an antibiotic soap, followed by a topical ointment and antibiotics.

Stud Tail is a condition that occurs when the skin's sebaceous glands near the base of the tail are overactive, producing excessive oil that blocks the hair follicles and forms blackheads. More common in breeding males, it is also seen in neutered males and female cats. Treatment includes cleaning the skin, application of topical medications, antibiotics and shaving the hair.

Rodent Ulcer, sometimes called an eosinophilic ulcer, appears as a small sore on the margin of the cat's lower lip. While unsightly, a rodent ulcer is not painful and usually responds well to an injection of corticosteroid.

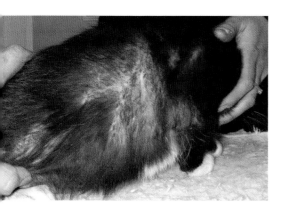

Allergic Dermatitis is a skin disease caused by an allergic reaction, which can result in itching and hair loss.

Common Ailments

Vomiting is a symptom that may be caused by disease,

◄ This cat is suffering from a form of allergic dermatitis, a skin condition that has a variety of causes.

► Vomiting in cats can be a symptom of many things; if it persists for long periods, consult your vet.

excitement, obstruction, parasites, poor liver and kidney function and poisoning. If a cat has persistent vomiting and you know it has not eaten poison, withdraw food for 12–24 hours and limit water intake. If the vomiting persists, consult your vet.

Diarrhoea can be an indication of parasites, poor diet, tumours, injury or chemical irritants. True diarrhoea is watery or bloody. Treatment includes a change of diet and medication to help solidify the bowel movements.

Constipation, which is infrequent or difficult bowel movements, is caused by little exercise, poor diet, hairballs, intestinal blockage or tumours. Symptoms include lethargy, poor appetite, distended abdomen and hard faeces. Treatment includes adding roughage to the diet or administering a laxative or enema to move the blockage.

Halitosis or bad breath may be caused by certain foods, intestinal disturbances, urinary ailments or infections of the teeth and mouth.

Diabetes can affect a cat of any age but is more common in older or overweight felines. It results from high blood glucose (sugar) levels caused by an insulin deficiency. Symptoms include increased thirst and appetite with accompanying weight loss. Diagnosis is confirmed by blood and urine tests. Treatment includes insulin injections and feeding a carbohydrate /sugar-restricted diet.

◀ Constipation can be treated by introducing roughage to your cat's diet or administering a laxative.

▶ Diabetes is caused by an insulin deficiency; overweight cats are particularly prone to this illness.

Arthritis is the progressive deterioration of joint cartilage. Symptoms include stiffness, limping, reluctance to climb or jump.

Asthma is an allergic respiratory condition in cats resulting in sneezing, coughing, wheezing, and difficulty breathing. Symptoms can range from mild to life threatening.

Prolapsed Rectum occurs when part of the rectum is pushed outside the anus, usually due to straining with diarrhoea. It appears as a red tub hanging out the anus. It requires surgery as soon as possible.

Cataracts are more common in older cats. They cause cloudiness in the lens, leading to poor vision or blindness.

More Serious Ailments

Gastritis is a general term used to describe inflammation of the lining of the stomach. The main symptom is vomiting, although it may be mild and self-limiting or so severe as to be life threatening, necessitating hospitalization and intensive supportive care.

Calicivirus is a contagious upper respiratory infection spread by direct contact with an infected cat or object. Symptoms include sneezing and coughing with discharge

◄ Excessive salivation or foaming at the mouth can indicate a variety of ailments.

► Fatigue and exercise intolerance in your cat could be a symptom of cardiomyopathy.

from the eyes and nose, fever and loss of appetite. Calicivirus and FVR (see page 210) infections account for 95 per cent of upper respiratory infections in cats.

Cardiomyopathy is a disease of the heart, which results from either a very thickened heart muscle, resulting in very small heart chambers (hypertropic cardiomyopathy) or a stretched heart muscle with very large heart chambers (dilated cardiomyopathy). Both forms result in a heart that is unable to function properly in pumping blood throughout the body. Symptoms include shortness of breath, fatigue and exercise intolerance.

Heart Murmur occurs when there is turbulence in the flow of blood through the chambers of the heart, usually due to a faulty heart valve. Many kittens are born with murmurs and outgrow them later in life. Many cats with murmurs live long healthy lives. There is a small risk that murmurs can lead to congestive heart failure.

Pneumonia may be caused by a virus or bacteria, as a primary infection or secondary to another disease, such as enteritis. Symptoms include a harsh cough, thick, often bloody nasal discharge, raspy laboured breathing and fever. Treatment includes antibiotics and support therapy. Pleurisy is a common complication that causes the cat to breathe heavily and be short of breath.

Chlamydia is highly contagious. Symptoms include inflammation of the eyes and nasal passages, sneezing, ocular discharge, nasal drainage, tearing and salivation and coughing. It may be transmitted to humans. Specific antibiotics are effective.

◀ Weight loss can have many causes, but in an older cat it could be a symptom of hyperthyroidism.

Cystitis is an acute or chronic inflammation of the bladder caused by stones or infection, and can be painful and debilitating. Cystitis may exist as a primary ailment or as a complication of another disease. Symptoms of cystitis include frequent urination, straining, pain, bloody urine, vomiting and bloating.

Ear Hematoma is an accumulation of blood between the skin and the ear cartilage, often following an injury from head shaking caused by an ear infection. Symptoms include pawing at the ear, shaking the head, a soft swelling inside or outside the ear, pain or sensitivity when touched and heat in the affected parts. Surgical drainage is required.

Hyperthyroidism is a common disease in middle age to older cats caused by excessive secretion of thyroid hormone. Symptoms include weight loss, enormous appetite, poor hair coat, hyperactivity, heavy breathing, coughing, vomiting and diarrhoea.

Impacted Anal Glands result when the two secretory organs located on either side of the anus become blocked. Symptoms include excessive licking or dragging of the rear end (scooting). In severe cases, the anal gland may abscess.

Inflammatory Bowel Disease (IBD) is a chronic disease of the gastro-intestinal tract. It can be a frustrating disease and frequently causes vomiting and diarrhoea for affected cats. Food allergies, chronic bacterial infection or autoimmune disorders may play a role.

Keratitis is an inflammation or ulceration of the cornea of the eye usually resulting from an injury. Symptoms include sensitivity to light and occasionally a bluish white clouding of the eye. The treatment is similar to that for conjunctivitis. It can progress if not treated.

▶ A kitten suffering from conjunctivitis – an inflammation of the membrane lining the eyelid and eyeball.

Conjunctivitis is an inflammation of the membrane lining the inner surface of the eyelids and the front part of the eyeball. Symptoms include redness, squinting and sensitivity to light. It may be caused by irritants, injury, disease or a foreign body in the eye. Provide some relief by washing the eye with warm water. Treatment depends of cause but may include antibiotic eye drops.

Pneumonitis is a highly contagious virus resembling the common head cold in human beings. The incubation period ranges from six to ten days with symptoms lasting as long as six weeks. Symptoms include running eyes, nasal discharge, sneezing fits and salivation. Though rarely fatal, secondary infections are common. Treatment includes antihistamines, antibiotics, cleaning the eyes and nose and applying eye ointment. The effectiveness of the pneumonitis vaccine is limited, protecting the cat for about six months at most and is only recommended if a cat is in a high-risk situation.

Potentially Fatal Illnesses

Feline Immunodeficiency Virus (FIV) also called Feline AIDS is a contagious viral disease spread through contact with an infected cat, with wounds sustained while fighting being a common means of infection. It is

a serious, often fatal disease that suppresses the immune system. This virus only affects cats, and is not transmittable to humans. Symptoms include chronic infections or bouts of illness, anorexia, diarrhoea, vomiting, pale mucous membranes, and chronic fever. FIV positive cats should be isolated from other cats to prevent spreading the disease.

◀ If your cat's eyes are weepy, it could be sign that it has an eye infection.

▶ FIV is a contagious disease, commonly contracted as a result of fighting with an infected cat.

Feline Infectious Anaemia (FIA) is caused by a microscopic parasite that attaches to the red blood cells and destroys them, causing low red blood cell count.

Feline Infectious Peritonitis (FIP) is a highly contagious virus spread via urine, faeces, and saliva. The wet form is characterized by an enlarged abdomen filled with fluid. Other symptoms include anorexia, depression, weight loss and dehydration. The dry form has similar symptoms along with lesions on the eyes. FIP can be hard to diagnose and cats who contract this virus rarely survive.

Cancer All types of cancer are found in the cat including cancer of the skin, mammary glands, bones, blood and blood tissues. Symptoms include lumps on the skin or bleeding from the rectum or reproductive organs. Older cats especially should be examined regularly by a vet for symptoms of an early cancer. Many cancers can be cured if diagnosed early.

Feline Leukaemia (FeLV) is a highly contagious virus spread via saliva, urine, tears, and milk most often contracted through fighting or as a nursing kitten. There is no cure. Exposed cats may not develop symptoms but become carriers, spreading the disease to other cats. The virus suppresses the immune system, causes severe anaemia, and cancer. Symptoms include fever, anorexia, weight loss, and anaemia. Testing is recommended as part of routine preventive cat health care programme. Vaccination is recommended for those cats at high risk such as outdoor cats. A positive cat should live as an indoor only cat so as not to spread the disease to other cats.

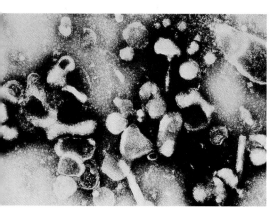

◀ The feline leukaemia virus (FeLV), which is highly contagious and can prove fatal.

▶ Cat flu is an airborne virus and results in sneezing, coughing, fever and loss of appetite.

Feline Lower Urinary Tract Disease (FLUTD), sometimes called Feline Urologic Syndrome (FUS), is a collection of diseases that affect the urinary system of the cat. Male cats suffering from FLUTD can develop a life-threatening obstruction of the urinary tract called a blocked bladder. Symptoms include poor litter tray habits, excessive licking of the genitals and incontinence.

Blocked Bladder occurs when material, usually bladder stones, prevents urine from exiting the bladder. The cat's bladder becomes distended and sensitive to the touch. If not relieved, the cat will become toxic and death may follow within forty-eight hours. Prompt veterinary attention is necessary.

Feline Viral Rhinotracheitis (FVR) also called 'cat flu', is a highly contagious airborne upper respiratory virus. Symptoms include sneezing and coughing with discharge from the eyes and nose, fever and loss of appetite. Young kittens and elderly cats are more susceptible and many require hospitalization to recover.

Upper Respiratory Infection (URI) is common, especially in young cats. Symptoms of URI include sneezing, coughing, runny eyes, runny nose, lack of appetite and wheezing. Vaccination against calicivirus and feline rhinotracheitis (feline herpes virus) should be part of a preventive cat health-care programme, as these diseases are frequent causes of upper respiratory infections in cats.

Kidney Disease is common in senior cats. Symptoms include excessive thirst and urination, lack of appetite, vomiting, and lethargy.

Panleukopenia, also known as feline distemper, is a highly contagious viral disease spread by contact with infected animals or their secretions. Symptoms include vomiting, diarrhoea, weakness, dehydration, tremors, loss of coordination and low white blood cells. Cats need to be hospitalized and have intensive care. Mortality rate is high.

▶ Cats suffering from panleukopenia need intensive treatment and therefore must be hospitalized.

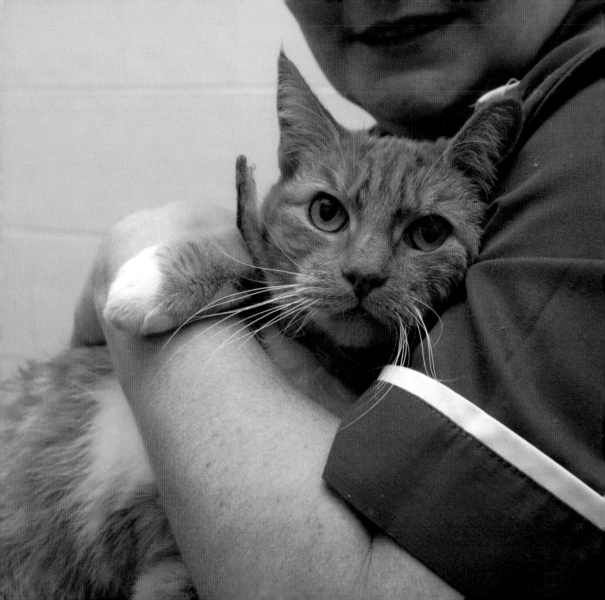

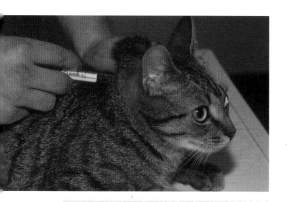

▲ There is no known cure for rabies, but your cat can be vaccinated against it.

Rabies Rabies is a virus that affects the nervous system and is always fatal. There is no known cure. Symptoms include behaviour change, difficulty swallowing, excessive salivation, depression, eventual stupor and hind limb paralysis. The disease is spread through the saliva of infected animals and can be transmitted through a bite or an open wound. Vaccinated pets exposed to rabies should be re-vaccinated and observed for 90 days. Un-vaccinated pets exposed to rabies should be isolated for 6 months. Rabies vaccination is an essential part of a preventive cat health care programme and many communities have laws requiring the vaccination of pets against rabies.

Vaccine Associated Sarcoma is a tumour that develops at the site of a vaccine injection. Because it is difficult to surgically remove a tumor in the shoulder area, most vets vaccinate in the hip area rather than in the scruff of the neck.

Feline Injuries and First Aid

No matter how well you attempt to keep your cat safe, there is always the possibility that an accident may occur. Knowledge of basic cat first aid combined with a well-stocked feline first aid kit may save your cat's life in an emergency. Do not forget to keep the phone number of the vet and emergency clinic in the first aid kit.

▶ Bandages, in a range of sizes, are a key component of any feline first aid kit.

The Feline First Aid Kit – Medicines and Ointments

- Wound disinfectant such as Betadine or Nolvasan
- Triple antibiotic ointment for skin
- Antibiotic ophthalmic ointment for eyes, such as Terramycin
- Eye wash solution
- Sterile saline
- Anti-diarrhoea medicine
- Cat laxative in paste form
- Diphenhydramine (Benadryl) for allergic reactions
- Cortisone spray or cream to reduce itching
- Ear-cleaning solution
- Hydrogen peroxide used to make a pet vomit
- Activated charcoal to absorb ingested poisons
- Medicinal alcohol
- Hairball remedy
- Petroleum jelly

The Feline First Aid Kit – Bandages

- 7.5 cm sq (3 in sq) sterile, non-stick gauze pad
- 2.5 cm (1 in) and 5 cm (2 in) rolls of gauze bandage
- 2.5 cm (1 in) and 5 cm (2 in) rolls of elastic adhesive tape
- Cloth strips
- Cotton swabs and Cotton buds

▶ A feline first aid kit should include items such as tweezers, dressings, an eye dropper and blunt-tip scissors.

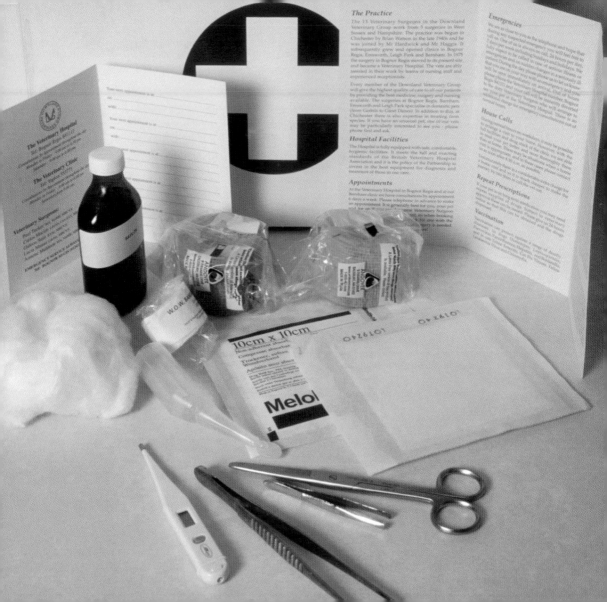

The Feline First Aid Kit – Tools

▶ Digital Rectal Thermometer
▶ Muzzle
▶ Short blade, blunt tip scissors
▶ Tweezers
▶ Nail clipper
▶ Metal fine-toothed comb
▶ Disposable syringe/eye dropper

Feline First Aid

Artificial Respiration If the cat has stopped breathing, lay it on its side on a flat surface. Open the mouth. If an object is blocking the airway, grab the tongue and pull it outward. Use fingers, surgical pliers, or a hemostat to pull it out. Once the airway is clear, lift the chin to straighten out the throat. Use one hand to grasp the muzzle and hold the mouth shut. Put your mouth completely over the nose and blow gently; the chest should expand. Blow just enough to move the chest. Wait for the air to leave the lungs before breathing again. Continue giving 20 breaths per minute, until the cat breathes on its own.

Bleeding Minor bleeding will stop on its own, however if the bleeding is more serious apply a cold-water compress then a pressure bandage of gauze and secure it with tape. If bleeding from a leg or tail is profuse, apply a tourniquet by tying a strip of cloth between the wound and the body. Rush to the vet.

Broken Bones If your cat has sustained a broken leg, fold a thin towel snugly around the injured limb and secure it in place or simply place the folded towel beneath the injured limb to provide support

▶ If your cat has a broken limb it is best to try and hold it in place until professional help can be given.

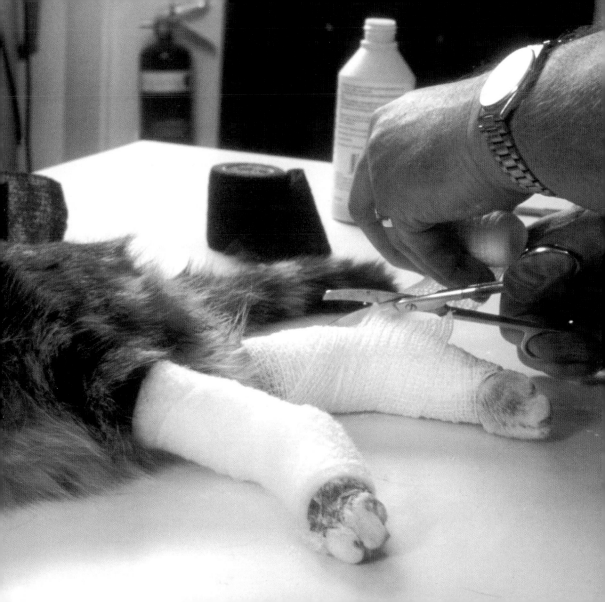

during transportation. Do not try to set the fracture or apply anything on an open wound. Keep the cat warm to prevent shock.

Burns A superficial burn appears red in colour and blisters, while a deeper, more serious burn will appear whitish. Immediately apply ice or cold water to a minor burn for 20 minutes. Serious burns require immediate veterinary attention.

CPR If your cat's heart has stopped beating, lay your cat on its side on a flat surface. Place the palm of your hand on the rib cage over the heart. Place your other hand on top of the first. For kittens, put your thumb on one side of the chest and the rest of your fingers on the other side. Compress the chest about one inch. Squeeze and release rhythmically at a rate of 80 to 100 compressions per minute. If also performing artificial respiration, alternate one breath with five compressions.

Drowning If you find your cat or kitten in water, apparently lifeless, make sure the airway is clear then hold the cat by the hind legs, swinging it upside down, back and forth between your legs to force water out of the lungs by centrifugal force.

Electric Shock Cats chewing on electrical wires may receive an electrical shock. If the cat is unconscious, check for a heartbeat by feeling the chest just behind the foreleg, perform CPR if necessary then rush the cat to the vet. Check the mouth and tongue for electrical burns as it will require medical attention.

▶ Though cats can swim, they may struggle to climb back out of deep-sided ponds and pools if they fall in.

◀ Paleness of the gums is one of the symptoms a vet will look for in a cat that may be suffering from shock.

Insect Bites and Stings Cats are fascinated by bugs. Paws and mouths are the most common location for an insect bite or sting. Symptoms include swelling and allergic response. Remove stinger, apply ice, administer an anti-histamine and seek veterinary care.

Poisoning If you know your cat has eaten something poisonous, but not caustic, induce vomiting by feeding 5 ml (one teaspoon) of 3 per cent hydrogen peroxide every 10 minutes until the cat begins to vomit.

Trauma/Shock Symptoms of shock include pale gums, rapid heartbeat, glassy eyes and cold, clammy skin. Keep warm and rush to vet.

Treatment and Medication

Choosing Your Vet

A vet is your partner in the health care of your cat. A good vet can be hard to find, so make sure you find one before you need one. You should have confidence in your vet's medical knowledge and you must be able to communicate well and feel comfortable with them. To find the one that best suits you and your feline friend consider what you want in a vet. The vet should be an experienced diagnostician competent in the latest veterinary procedures and interested in cat-specific medicine. Ideally the veterinary hospital should be a clean, well-maintained facility in a nearby location with available parking, convenient office hours and easy payment procedures. Is there a separate facility for feline patients away from the dogs? What is the range of services that the veterinary hospital provides? Is there an on-site x-ray machine, in-house laboratory facilities, ultrasound machine, laser, dental x-ray machine or endoscope? Ask about training and experience with high-tech machines and procedures. Is there an emergency service? If the practice has

▶ Cats cannot resist catching insects, but this can result in bites or stings to the mouth and paws.

multiple vets, can you specify which vet will treat your cat? Does the vet have a speciality such as surgery, dental care, eye care or allergies? Are the support staff friendly and helpful?

To find a good vet, ask for recommendations from cat owners in your area, groomers or a local pet store. When moving, ask your former vet if he can recommend a vet in your new hometown. When receiving a recommendation, ask why they like that particular vet. The 'why' is as important as the recommendation.

Some owners prefer a 'cats only' vet who concentrates all their efforts on feline-specific issues. A general small animal practice may still be a better choice if the attitude of the vet and facilities better suit your needs.

Once you have narrowed your list of recommendations to conveniently located vets with office hours, payment policies and emergency procedures that meet your needs, visit the hospitals and take a tour. No one vet or facility is likely to perfectly meet all your needs, so decide what your priorities are. Once you have made your choice, make an appointment for the vet to see your cat for an initial checkup.

Home Care

Once a sick cat has been examined by a vet, diagnosed, treated and returns home, it is important to keep it warm, quiet, well fed, watered and to follow-up on medications or treatment the vet recommends.

Taking Your Cat's Temperature

A cat's normal rectal temperature is 38.1–39.2 °C (100.5–102.5 °F). Sphynx and Rex breeds may have a slightly higher normal temperature of 39–39.5 °C (102–103 °F). Feeling the ears, nose or head is not considered a reliable method to determine temperature.

▶ A rectal thermometer is the most reliable way of checking your cat's body temperature.

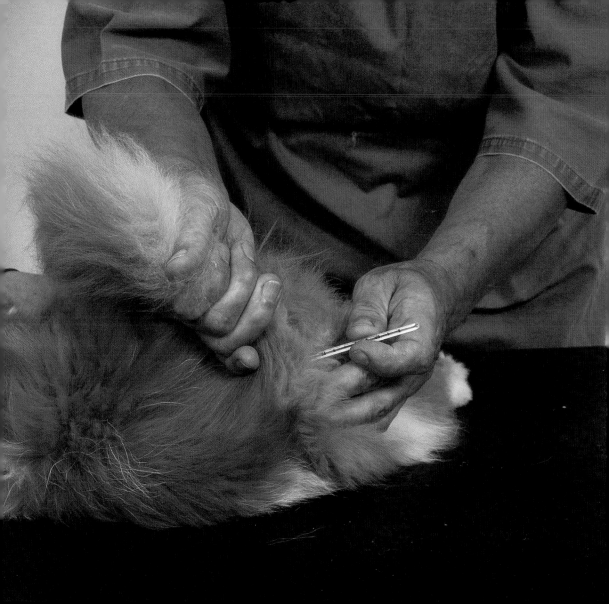

The easiest thermometer to use is a digital rectal thermometer. Choose one with a flexible tip. Coat the tip with petroleum jelly. Place the standing cat on a counter, hugging its body to yours. Grasp the tail at the base and raise it, holding it firmly so the cat will not sit down. Gently insert the bulb portion of the thermometer into the anus using a twisting motion. Insert the thermometer about 1 inch leaving it in place until the thermometer beeps. Remove the thermometer and read the temperature. A high temperature could indicate an infection. A temperature below normal may indicate shock.

Ear thermometers can also be used in cats. They are generally fast and easy but it is essential to use a proper technique to obtain an accurate reading. The normal ear temperature in cats is 37.8–39.4 ˚C (100.0 –103.0 ˚F). The ear thermometer works by measuring infrared heat waves that come from the eardrum, so it is important to place the thermometer deep into the horizontal ear canal. The first few times you use it, take both ear and rectal temperatures and compare. The results should be very close.

Taking Your Cat's Pulse

To take a cat's pulse, use light fingertip pressure on the inside of the cat's thigh where the femoral artery can be felt. The femoral artery pulsation determines the pulse rate. A normal rate is about 110 to 135 beats per minute, varying with age, exercise, excitement and condition of the cat. Respiration should be 25 to 40 per minute. In shock, the pulse is very fast and weak.

Taking Your Cat's Heartbeat

In a difficult situation where you cannot take the pulse by touch, it may be possible to observe the heartbeat by watching or feeling the chest. One rise plus one fall equals one breath. Cats at rest take about 30–50 breaths per minute.

▶ Vets check a cat's heartbeat using a stethoscope, but there are ways in which you can check this yourself.

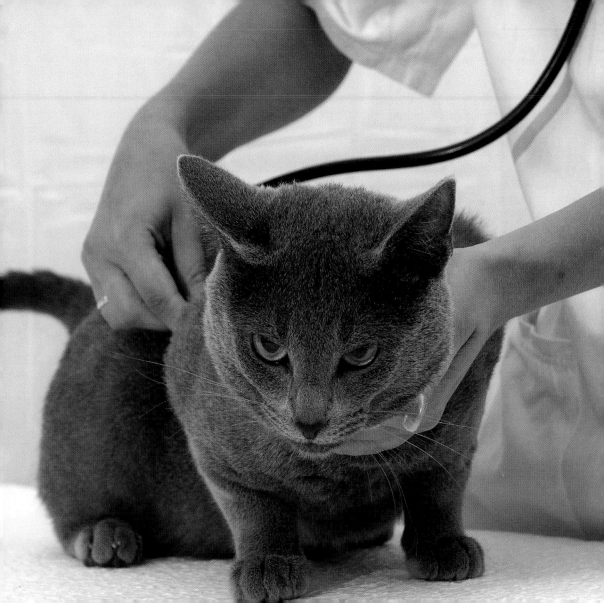

Giving Your Cat a Pill

Place the cat on the kitchen counter or alternately sitting on your lap. If un-cooperative, wrap the cat tightly in a towel, leaving only his head visible. Hold the cat's head from the top using your left hand if you are right-handed. The cat's cheekbones provide a convenient handle by which to hold the head firmly without causing the cat any discomfort. Tilt the head back and the cat will often drop its lower jaw open. Force the mouth open by squeezing your thumb and finger together and applying gentle pressure at the corners of the cat's mouth. Hold the pill or capsule in your right hand between your index finger and thumb. You can place one of the remaining fingers of your right hand on the lower incisors to keep the lower jaw open. Drop the pill or capsule as far back on the tongue as possible. You can also use your forefinger to poke the pill gently down the throat. Close the mouth and blow on the cat's face to encourage it to swallow. Stroke the neck and throat while holding the mouth closed.

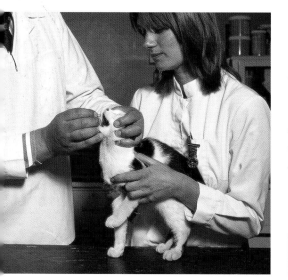

Give the cat a small quick toss in the air. The cat gulps, and the pill goes down.

It is recommended that whenever giving your cat a pill or capsule you always follow it immediately by syringing several cc's of water into the cat's mouth to help the medication 'go down'. Giving your cat a drink of water after giving it a medication in either pill or capsule form helps the pill reach the stomach faster. Also, give him a favourite treat – baby food or fresh meat perhaps – so he associates pill taking with a pleasant experience.

◄ If your cat is not amenable to taking pills, it may help to have someone else hold it still.

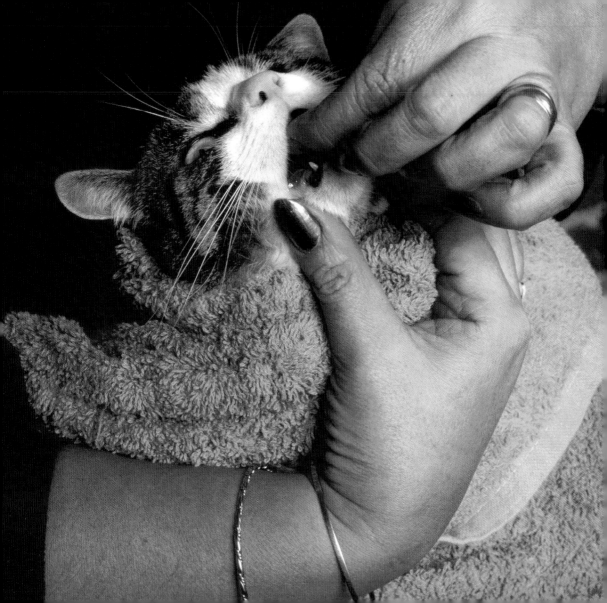

Pill Poppers The pill popper (or 'piller') is used to administer tablets and capsules safely, quickly, and easily. It is a syringe-type plastic instrument that consists of a long plastic barrel with a plastic plunger, plus a rubber flexible tip. The rubber tip is split to hold pills better. The soft rubber is gentle to the inside of the cat's mouth and holds the tablet firmly.

Place the medication in the rubber tip of the piller. Tip the cat's head back and open the mouth slightly. In one quick motion place the rubber tip of the piller as far as possible behind the root of the tongue. In the same motion push the plunger to empty the piller. Withdraw the piller and close the cat's mouth. Rub the throat until you see the cat swallow.

The rubber tip degrades over time. This can create a risk of it actually falling off in the cat's mouth and being accidentally swallowed. Check the rubber tip for cracks or a slight colour change.

Administering Eye Drops

If the cat is difficult to handle, wrap it tightly in a towel. Place the cat on a table or worktop. If you are right-handed, hold the cat's head with the nose pointed slightly up with your left hand. Your right hand holds the dropper bottle. Place the outer edge of your hand on top of the cat's head with the tip of the dropper bottle aimed for the correct eye and pull back to open up the eyelid fully. Putting your hand on top of the animal's head will help prevent accidentally poking the eye with the bottle. One or

◄ An experienced vet can apply eye ointment straight from the tube, but it may be safer to use a clean finger.

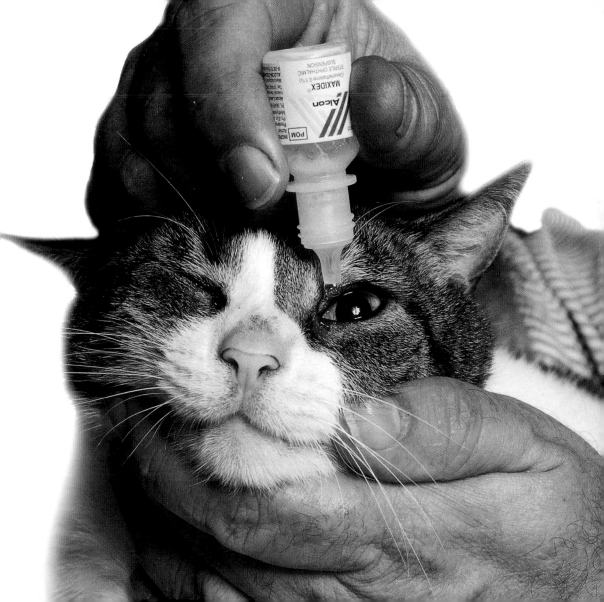

two drops are enough. Repeat with the other eye if needed. Never hold the eye dropper so that the tip can touch the eye as the medication may become contaminated. Also if the animal moves suddenly, the tip may poke into the pet's eye and cause significant damage.

Administering Eye Ointment

The safest way to administer ointment into the eye is using your finger. The tube tips are usually fairly pointy and can do a lot of damage if accidentally touched to the eye, or the ointment may become contaminated from contact with an infected eye. Wash your hands, and try not to touch anything with your right index finger. With the animal restrained, place a short strip (about 1 cm ($^2/_5$ in) of ointment on the tip of your right index finger. With your other hand and fingers, open up the eyelid and 'scrape' the ointment from your finger onto the inside surface of the lower lid. Then close the lids and rub them around to distribute the ointment.

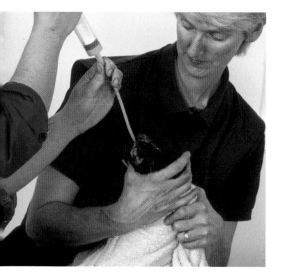

Administering Ear Drops

Tip the cat's head slightly and insert the drops as far down the ear canal as possible. Gently massage for several minutes. If the drops need to be refrigerated, allow them to reach room temperature before using.

Force Feeding

A sick cat may stop eating. If the cat stops eating for more than a day, it is critical that it be forced to eat. High-calorie

◄ If a cat refuses to eat for more than one day, it becomes necessary to try force-feeding.

supplements are available in tubes. Place an inch on your finger then force the cat's mouth open, place far back on tongue and hold the cat's mouth closed until it swallows. Liquefied food can be placed in a large syringe and force fed by placing the tip in the side of the mouth. Keep the cat hydrated by syringing unflavoured rehydration formula or water.

The Elizabethan Collar

An Elizabethan collar is a truncated cone-shaped device that fits over the head of the cat to prevent the animal from biting or licking at its body or scratching at its head or neck while wounds or injuries heal. It is attached to the cat's collar with strings or tabs passed through holes punched in the sides of the plastic. The neck of the collar should be short enough to let the cat eat and drink. Collars can be bought from vets or pet stores.

Caring For the Elderly Cat

Advances in modern veterinary medicine and nutrition have extended the average life expectancy of a cat to almost 15 years, with many reaching 20 years and beyond. With increased longevity come concerns regarding the special needs of the senior citizen feline.

Although the common belief is one cat year equals seven years in human terms, cats actually age fastest

▶ Cats with wounds that need to heal without being licked or scratched may be fitted with an Elizabethan collar.

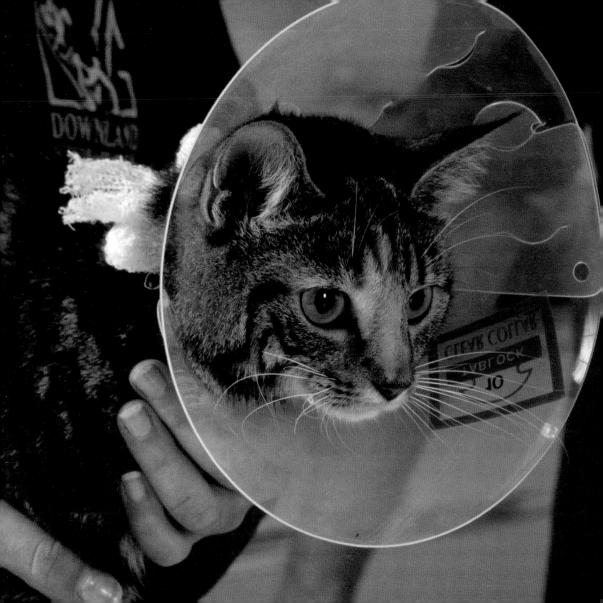

in their first year. A 12–18-month-old cat is roughly equivalent to a 20-year-old human. By two years of age, the rate of maturing slows until each year is equivalent to four human years. A ten-year-old cat is equivalent to a person in their mid-50s. Some cats encounter age-related problems as young as seven years of age while most felines show definite signs of aging by 12 years of age.

Special Needs of the Older Cat

A cat sleeps more as it ages. Because it grooms itself less, its coat may begin to look greasy, tangled and have an odour. The claws may become thick and brittle. The skin grows thinner and less elastic. More frequent bathing, combing and nail trimming may help prevent hairballs, matting and skin problems, particularly for longhaired cats.

The older cat often feels cold more keenly. A heating pad or a cat sweater may make it more comfortable. Arthritis is common. Signs include a cat that moves more slowly, seems reluctant to climb or hesitates when jumping down. It may have difficulty climbing into the litter tray or using stairs so add extra litter trays, food and water in various locations in the home, especially on each level of a multi-storey home.

Some loss of hearing or vision is not uncommon in an older cat; however neither seems to bother most cats as long as they are in familiar surroundings. Loss of ability to smell may result in poor appetite, so a more smelly, appetizing food may need to be offered. If the cat is too thin, it needs a diet with higher calorie count per cup. If gaining weight, consider a low fat, high protein diet.

Bad breath, drooling or reluctance to eat may signal dental problems such as tartar, gingivitis or tooth decay. Don't be too concerned if the cat must have teeth removed as most cats manage fine with missing teeth. Soft foods and more frequent, smaller meals may help. The older cat may develop problems with incontinence, diarrhoea or constipation, possibly related to kidney problems or diabetes. Commercial diets are available formulated for the special nutritional needs of the older cat or the cat with medical issues.

Elderly cats can develop symptoms similar to human Alzheimer's. Behaviours can include wandering, excessive meowing, staring at walls and disorientation. Medications are available that may help. Stress should be kept at a minimum for the elderly cat. If a senior cat displays signs of illness, it should be addressed immediately as any problem is more likely to have a detrimental effect on the aging pet. While many vets no longer recommend yearly booster vaccinations for their older clients, a physical and dental checkup should be performed annually. Some signs of ageing are also signs of poor health so never simply assume that changes you see in your older cat are to old age, and therefore untreatable.

Euthanasia

There may come a time in a cat owner's life when there is a need for great love and perhaps greater courage. When injury, illness or old age makes a cat's life too painful to continue, the option of euthanasia must be considered. Euthanasia is accomplished by injecting a large overdose of a very powerful anesthetic. The cat slips into a quiet, irreversible deep unconsciousness. Death comes quickly and painlessly. The sense of loss after the death of a pet can be as profound as the loss of a human family member. If you feel overwhelmed by a sense of guilt or sadness, there are online grief counselling websites to help you deal with the loss of a pet.

◄ Placing a memorial in a pet cemetery can help some people to overcome the death of a beloved pet.

Useful Addresses

Cat Registries and Organisations

The Governing Council of the Cat Fancy (GCCF)
5 King's Castle Business Park
The Drove
Bridgwater
Somerset, TA6 4AG
UK
Tel: +44 (0)1278 427 575
www.gccfcats.org

Fédération Internationale Féline (FIFe)
www.fifeweb.org

Co-ordinating Cat Council of Australia (CCC of A)
Secretary
P.O. Box 347
Macedon, Victoria 3440
Australia
Tel: +61 (0)3 5426 1758
http://cccofa.asn.au/

New Zealand Cat Fancy (NZCF)
Membership Coordinator
264 Cannon Hill Crescent
Christchurch 8008
New Zealand
www.nzcatfancy.gen.nz

Cat Fanciers' Association (CFA)
PO Box 1005
Manasquan, New Jersey 08736
USA
Tel: +1 980 528 9797
www.cfainc.org

American Cat Fanciers Association (ACFA)
PO Box 1949
Nixa, Missouri 65714
USA
Tel: +1 417 725 1530
www.acfacat.com

The International Cat Association (TICA)
P.O. Box 2684
Harlingen, Texas 78551
USA
Tel: +1 956 428 8046
www.ticaeo.org

Cat Fanciers' Federation (CFF)
PO Box 661
Gratis, Ohio 45330
USA
Tel: +1 937 787 9009
www.cffinc.org

Canadian Cat Association (CCA)
289 Rutherford Road, S #18
Brampton, ON
L6W 3R9 Canada
Tel: +1 905 459 1481
www.cca-afc.com

International Society for Endangered Cats
124 Lynnbrook Road SE
Calgary, Alberta T2C 1S6
Canada
Tel: +1 403 279 589
www.wildcatconservation.org

American Association of Cat Enthusiasts
PO Box 213
Pine Brook,
New Jersey 07058
USA
Tel: +1 973 335 6717
www.aaceinc.org

Feline Conservation Federation
7816 N. County Road 75 W
Shelburn,
Indiana 47879
USA
www.felineconservation.org

International Progressive Cat Breeders' Alliance
PO Box 311
Upton,
Kentucky 42784
USA
Tel: +1 270 531 7966
www.ipcba.8k.com

Welfare and Rescue Organisations

Royal Society for the Prevention of Cruelty to Animals
Wilberforce Way
Southwater
Horsham
West Sussex, RH13 9RS
UK
Tel: +44 (0)300 1234 999
www.rspca.org.uk

Cats Protection
National Cat Centre
Chelwood Gate
Haywards Heath
Sussex, RH17 7TT
UK
Tel: +44 (0)8702 099 099
www.cats.org.uk

The Original Cat Action Trust
The Old Smithy
Rattery, South Brent
Devon, TQ10 9LE
UK
www.catactiontrust.org.uk

American Humane Association
63 Inverness Drive East
Englewood, Colorado 80112
USA
Tel: +1 303 792 9900
www.americanhumane.org

The Humane Society of the United States
2100 L Street NW
Washington, D.C. 20037
USA
Tel: +1 202 452 1100
www.hsus.org

Big Cat Rescue
12802 Easy Street
Tampa, Florida 33625
USA
Tel: +1 813 920 4130
www.bigcatrescue.org

Advice and Information

Feline Advisory Bureau
Taeselbury, High Street
Tisbury, Wiltshire, SP3 6LD
UK
Tel: +44 (0)870 742 2278
www.fabcats.org

Cat World Magazine
Ancient Lights, 19 River Road
Arundel
West Sussex, BN18 9EY
UK
Tel: +44 (0)1903 884 988
www.catworld.co.uk

Pet Website
18 Shepherds Close
Grove
Oxfordshire, OX12 0NX
UK
www.petwebsite.com/cats

Cat Channel
477 Butterfield,
Suite 200
Lombard, Illinois 60148
USA
Tel: +1 630 515 9493
www.catchannel.com

Cats International
193 Granville Road
Cedarburg
Wisconsin 53012
USA
Tel: +1 262 375 8852
www.catsinternational.org

Pet Place
20283 State Road 7,
Suite 400
Boca Raton
FL 33498
USA
Tel: +1 561 237 2940
www.petplace.com

Show Cats Online
PO Box 4971
Blaine
Washington 98231-4971
USA
Tel: +1 604-535-7469
www.showcatsonline.com

Terrific Cats
PO Box 15124
New Bern
North Carolina 28561
USA
www.terrific-cats.com

Further Reading

Altman, Roberta, *The Quintessential Cat*, Hungry Minds Inc. (New York, New York), 1996

Bard, E.M., *Test Your Cat: The Cat IQ Test*, HarperCollins (New York, New York), 2005

Becker, Marty; and Spadafori, Gina, *Why Do Cats Always Land on Their Feet?: 101 of the Most Perplexing Questions Answered about Feline Unfathomables, Medical Mysteries, and Befuddling Behaviors*, HCI (Deerfield Beach, Florida), 2006

Bessant, Claire, *The Cat Whisperer*, Blake Publishing (London, UK), 2004

Burn, David, *An Instant Guide to Cats*, Gramercy Books (New York, New York), 2000

Christensen, Wendy, *The Humane Society of the United States Complete Guide to Cat Care*, St Martin's Griffin (New York, New York), 2004

Choron, Sandra and Harry, *Planet Cat: A CAT-olog*, Houghton Mifflin, 2007

Church, Christine, *House Cat: How to Keep Your Indoor Cat Sane and Sound*, John Wiley & Sons (Somerset, New Jersey), 2005

Cutts, Paddy, *The Complete Cat Book: An Encyclopedia of Cats, Cat Breeds & Cat Care*, Lorenz Books (London, UK), 2000

Edgar, Jim, *Bad Cat*, Hodder & Stoughton (London, UK), 2007

Edwards, Alan, *The Ultimate Encyclopedia of Cats*, Lorenz Books (London, UK), 2003

Elliot, Charles, *The Cat Fanatic: Quirky Quotes on Frisky Felines*, JR Books Ltd (London, UK), 2007

Elridge, Debra; Carlson, Delbert; Carlson, Lisa; and Griffin, James, *Cat Owner's Home Veterinary Handbook*, John Wiley & Sons (Somerset, New Jersey), 2007

Fogle, Bruce, *The New Encyclopedia of the Cat*, Dorling Kindersley (London, UK), 2007

Halls, Vicky, *Cat Confidential*, Bantam Books Ltd (New York, New York), 2005

Hotchner, Tracie, *The Cat Bible: Everything Your Cat Expects You to Know*, Gotham (New York, New York), 2007

Johnson-Bennett, Pam, *Cat vs Cat: Keeping the Peace When You Have More Than One Cat*, Penguin (New York, New York), 2004

Johnson-Bennett, Pam, *Psycho Kitty: Tips for Solving Your Cat's Behaviour*, Celestial Arts (Berkley, California), 2008

Loxton, Howard, *Cats: 99 Lives: Cats in History, Legend and Literature*, Duncan Baird Publishers (London, UK), 2001

Malek, Jaromir, *The Cat in Ancient Egypt*, British Museum Press (London, UK), 2006

Neville, Peter; and Bessant, Claire, *The Perfect Kitten*, Hamlyn (London, UK), 2005

O'Neill, Amanda, *Cat Biz*, Barron's Educational Series (Hauppauge, New York), 2006

Pilbeam, Mavis, *The British Museum Little Book of Cats*, British Museum Press (London, UK), 2004

RSPCA, *Care For Your Cat*, HarperCollins (London, UK), 2006

Somerville, Louisa, *The Ultimate Guide to Cat Breeds*, Chartwell Books, 2007

Sunquist, Mel and Fiona, *Wild Cats of the World*, University of Chicago Press (Chicago, Illinois), 2002

Tabor, Roger, *Understanding Cat Behavior*, David & Charles Plc (Devon, UK), 2003

Verhoef-Verhallen, Esther, *The Complete Encyclopedia of Cats*, Chartwell Books, 2005

Zuffi, Stefano, *The Cat in Art*, Harry N. Abrams Inc. (New York, New York), 2007

Glossary

Accepted
A characteristic accepted in a breed standard.

ACFA
American Cat Fanciers Association.

Acute disease
A rapidly progressing illness.

Adult cat
Any cat over the age of eight months old in most cat registries for show purposes.

Agouti
Cat colour that results from each individual hair follicle having contrasting bands of colour.

Agouti gene
The gene that produces striping or a tabby pattern.

Ailurophile
A cat-loving person.

Ailurophobe
A person that hates cats.

Albino
A cat that is white because it lacks melanin pigmentation.

Allowable outcross
A cat that is allowed by a cat registry to be mated to another breed of cat in order to produce a kitten with certain favourable characteristics. The Abyssinian, for example, is an allowable outcross for the Somali.

Alopecia
Loss of hair, bald patches – usually due to illness.

Alter
To spay or neuter a cat.

Anoestrus
The condition of not being in season for a female cat.

AOC (any other colour)
Non-recognized accepted colour or pattern in a certain breed of cat.

AOV (any other variety)
Cat association term to classify cats that are offspring of registered parents, but are not eligible to enter championship cat show classes because they do not have the official requirements for coat colour, coat length or other physical characteristics.

Asymptomatic
Exhibiting no symptoms of a disease.

Autoimmune disease
The body's own defence mechanisms attack normal tissues.

Awn hairs
The part of the cat's undercoat that is longer than the downy undercoat but shorter than the primary guard coat.

Awry
Crooked jaw formation.

Back crossing
Inbreeding where a cat is mated with a parent.

Barring
Stripes associated with tabby markings.

Base coat

The primary coat.

Benched

When a cat is kept and displayed in a separate area to that where it is judged.

Benching cage

Show-hall cage where a cat is kept and displayed when it is not being judged.

Best in show

Most points and winner of a championship.

Best of breed

A cat, which in the judge's opinion, comes closest to meeting the breed standard among all other competing cats of that breed.

BEW

Blue-eyed white.

Bib

The part of the coat including the lower chin and the chest.

Bite

The angle at which the upper and lower teeth meet and intermesh.

Blaze

Stripe or splash of white on the cat's forehead or nose. (In blue-cream and tortoiseshell cats, a blaze is a vertical division of two colours (usually half red and half black) running down the middle of the face. 'Checkerboard' is the term used when this pattern is reversed on the cat's chin.

Bloodline

A cat's ancestry.

Blotched tabby

Another term for the classic or marbled tabby.

Boots

White markings on the hind paws or lower leg of a coloured cat. Also called 'gauntlets'.

Bracelets

Dark stripes on the legs of tabby-patterned cats.

Break

Well-pronounced angle between nose and forehead. Indentation on the bridge of the nose occurring between or near to the point between the eyes. Also called 'stop'.

Breeches

The longer hair on the back of the thighs of longhaired or semi-longhaired cats. Variant spelling of 'britches'.

Breed

A subdivision of the species consisting of individuals with common hereditary characteristics. Cats sharing common ancestors and similar physical characteristics.

Breed council

Cat association members who are actively involved in exhibiting and breeding cats of a specific breed.

Breed ribbon

An award for 'Best of Breed'.

Breed true

A breed is said to breed true when it produces kittens that have the same characteristics as their parents.

Brandling

A mingling of different coloured hairs in a coat.

Bronze

Egyptian Mau colour characterized by a rich, warm, red base colour with darker spotting and ticking.

Brush

The thick hair of the tail on a longhaired cat, especially Persian.

Bull's-eye
A mark found on the sides of the body of classic (blotched) tabby pattern cats that is characterized by a solid, circular spot of dark colouring surrounded by a ring of darker colouring.

Butterfly
Mark found on the shoulders of classic (blotched) tabby cat that resembles a butterfly.

Calling
The sound female cats make when they are interested in breeding.

Cameo
A type of cat colour that has a white base with red on the outer part of the hair shaft.

Carrier
A cat carrying a genetic defect or disease.

Castration
Removal of testicles in a male cat. (Neutering.)

Cat association
An organization for the promotion of cats, cat breeds, cat shows and cat health.

Cat Fancy
People who are involved in breeding, showing of cats and cat clubs.

Catnip
A plant of the mint family (*nepeta cataria*) that acts as a hallucinogen to cats.

Cattery
A place where cats are bred and raised. Alternately a facility for boarding cats.

Cattery name
The name of a cattery. Also used as the prefix or suffix of a registered cat's name, to indicate the breeder and/or owner.

CCA
Canadian Cat Association/Association Feline Canadienne.

CFA
Cat Fanciers' Association.

CFF
Cat Fanciers' Federation.

CEW
Copper-eyed white.

Champagne
Rich, soft beige colour found in the Burmese breed. American term for chocolate/lilac Burmese.

Champion
A title that is earned by a cat after accumulating a certain number of winner's points in cat shows. Considered as the first step towards becoming a Grand Champion. Some cat associations require six 'winners' ribbons for championship while others require a cat to 'final'.

Championship finals
Top ten pedigreed adult cats are awarded rosettes in the judging ring.

Championship status
Cats of a certain breed become eligible to compete for championship titles.

Checkerboard
Vertical division of two colours (usually half red and half black) running down the middle of the cat's chin.

Cherry eye
Prolapsed gland of the third eyelid.

Chestnut
Solid warm brown colour of cat.

Chinchilla
Cat that is white at the base with a small amount of darker colour on the tips. Lightest degree of tipping.

Chocolate
Light chestnut brown.

Chocolate lynx point
Medium chocolate brown coat with underlying tabby pattern.

Chocolate tortie point
Points primarily medium chocolate brown with additional tortoiseshell colours.

Cinnamon
Rich dark brownish red colour.

Classic tabby
A pattern with swirls and blotches of darker colour over a lighter base colour. Also called 'blotched' or 'marbled' tabby.

Closed cattery
A cattery that does not allow cats to come in or out, including for shows or stud service. Can also refer to simply not offering stud service to outside cats.

Coarse
A negative term for a cat that is not refined or harmonious in conformation.

Cobby
Body type typically massive, short, muscular, broad chest and hips, heavy boned and low on the legs.

Colitis
Inflammation of the large intestine.

Colour class
Divisions created by cat associations to classify certain types of coat colours or patterns, such as shaded colours or parti-colour.

Colostrum
Mother's milk secreted by the mother during the first few days following birth that provides the kittens with immunity to some diseases.

Concaveation
Spayed female cat produces milk in response to the suckling of a kitten.

Condition
Wellbeing of a cat, including muscle toning, grooming and good health.

Conformation
Structure of a cat's body, legs and tail.

Cottony
Refers to a coat that is long, fine and flyaway, such as on a Persian particularly.

Convex
Domed forehead.

CPC
Colourpoint Carrier, meaning that the cat carries the colourpoint gene.

Cream
Diluted version of red that appears as a pale beige colour.

Cream lynx point
Points that are cream to pale red with underlying tabby pattern.

Cross
Mating or breeding one cat with another.

Cryptorchid
A male with either one or both testicles not descended.

Dam
Female parent.

Dander
Scales of dead skin that can cause an allergic reaction in humans.

De-clawing
Surgically removing claws. A de-clawed cat is not allowed to enter competition.

Demodex
A mite that can cause mange.

Dewclaw
The first digit found on the inside of the leg above the front paws.

Dilute
A paler version of a primary colour. The dilute of black is blue and the dilute of red is cream.

Disqualification
Elimination from competition due to a serious fault.

Division
A cat show term that signifies a subdivision consisting of two or more colour classes.

DNA
Chemical substance that makes up chromosomes.

Domestic
A non-pedigreed cat.

Dominant
The prevailing gene member of a gene pair.

Doming
The rounded part of the head between the ears. Also refers to the rounded part of the forehead.

Down hairs
The shortest hair on the cat, soft and downy.

Dyslapsia
Abnormal development of a part of the cat's body.

Ear furnishings
Tufts of hair that grow in and around the ears.

Ear mites
Tiny insects that feed on the lining of the ear canal.

Ear tufts
Long hair originating from within the cup of the ear.

Ebony
Black.

Estrus
Being in heat. A period of varying length where a female cat produces a watery secretion from the genital tract and is sexually receptive to male cats. If mated, she will ovulate.

External parasites
Organisms such as ticks and mites that affect the outside areas of the body.

Fault
An imperfection or deviance from the breed standard.

Fawn
Pale buff, sandy, slightly pinkish tinge. Dilute of cinnamon.

Feline Immunodeficiency Virus (FIV)
Virus that attacks the cat's immune system.

Feline Infectious Peritonitis (FIP)
A coronavirus infection of the membrane lining the abdominal cavity. This disease leads to death.

Feline Leukaemia Virus (FeLV)
A virus that causes one of the most lethal infectious diseases found in cats. It is directly and indirectly the cause of many feline illnesses including cancer of the lymphocytes.

Feline Lower Urinary Tract Disease (FLUTD)
Urinary tract disease causing urethral blockage and kidney stone formation.

Feline Urologic Syndrome (FUS)
A disease of the urinary tract often responsible for blockage of the urethra in male cats. Life threatening.

Feral
Cats living in the wild.

Fever
Temperature in cats that is over 39°C (102°F).

Fillers
Material that is added to pet food in order to increase volume.

Follicle
The part of the skin from which hair grows.

Foreign
Term describing a fine-boned, long-limbed elegant cat such as a Siamese or Abyssinian.

Frill
A mass of long hair circling the neck, especially on a Persian, Also called 'ruff'.

Fungicidal
A product that prevents the growth of fungi.

Gauntlets
White markings on the hind paws or lower leg of a coloured cat. Also called 'boots'.

Gene
The individual hereditary units that control growth, development and the physical characteristics of a cat. They are found in specific locations on a chromosome.

Gene pool
Total of all the genes, dominant and recessive, that exist in a certain breed of cat.

Genetics
The science of heredity.

Genotype
Total of all the genes that a kitten inherits from its parents, recessive and dominant.

Gestation
Period of pregnancy. Cat pregnancy lasts between 63 and 69 days.

Ghost markings
Faint tabby striping or spots on a kitten's coat that disappear with maturity.

Gloves
Solid coloured markings, usually white, on the forepaws of a cat.

Gingivitis
Inflammation of the gums.

Goggles
The lighter coloured hair encircling the eyes. Also called 'spectacles'.

Grooming powder
A chalk-like powder used in grooming to give volume, separate the cat's hair and/or enhance the colour.

Ground colour
Hair colour that is closest to the body.

Guard hair
One of three types of hair in a cat's coat. Usually outer, longer and coarser than other hair.

Harlequin bicolour pattern
Predominantly white cat with several patches of colour scattered on the body.

Heat
The period where a female cat is receptive to mating.

Heterochromatic
Eyes of two different colours.

HHP
Household Pet.

Hip dysplasia
Hip socket malformation causing crippling in cats.

Hock
Cat's back-leg joint, similar to the human ankle.

Household pet
Domestic or purebred cat that is not registered and is a pet. Household pets can compete in special categories in cat shows.

Hot tortie/hot blue-cream
When colour is dominantly red or cream. Also called 'reverse tortie/reverse blue-cream'.

Hybrid
Result of mating cats of different breeds.

Hybrid vigor
Increased vitality resulting from breeding cats of two different breeds together.

IM
Intramuscular (injections).

Inbreeding
Mating of closely related individuals, usually brother to sister, mother to son or father to daughter.

Inherited
Characteristic that is the result of genetic influences.

Internal parasites
Larvae and worms that are living off the host cat's meals or its blood.

IV
Intravenous (injections).

Jacobson's Organ
A sensing organ in the top of the cat's mouth involved in smell and taste.

Jowls
Larger cheeks characteristic of unaltered, mature males.

Judging cage
Cage in the judging area.

Kitten
A cat up to the age of eight months old.

Laces
White area on back of hind legs from foot to hock, especially on Birman and Snowshoes. *See also* 'gauntlets', 'gloves'.

Lavender
Cat fur colour, grey with a pinkish cast.

Lilac-cream point
Points that are a mixture of lilac and cream.

Lilac-cream lynx point
Points that are a mixture of lilac and cream with an underlying tabby pattern.

Lilac lynx point
Points that are grey with a pinkish cast and that have an underlying tabby pattern.

Lilac point
Points that are grey with a pinkish cast.

Line breeding
Mating cats that are related by at least one common ancestor within the first three generations of their parents.

Litter
Kittens born in the same birth from the same mother.

Litter
Absorbent material used in a cat's tray.

Litter registration
Registering a litter of kittens with a cat registry organization, like the CFA or TICA.

Luxating patella
Genetically transmitted problem that causes the kneecap to slip when the joint is moved. Can cause lameness.

Lynx tip
Tuft of longer hair on the tip of ear, especially on a Maine Coon or Norwegian Forest Cat.

Lynx tufts
Hair furnishings on the tips of the ears.

Lynx point
Light body coat with darker extremities that have tabby markings. Also called 'tabby point'.

Mackerel
A tabby characterized by vertical stripes like a fish-bone pattern.

Mascara
Dark skin pigment found around the eye typical of silvers and tabbies.

Mask
Darker coloured area of face of a colourpoint.

Meezer
Slang term for a Siamese cat.

Melanin
Dark pigment produced by the body which gives colour to the skin, hair and eyes.

Metabolism
Physical and chemical processes that take place in a living being.

Mi-ke
Calico or tortoiseshell-and-white variety of Japanese Bobtail.

Mink
The result of the influence of point and sepia genes on the self gene (solid colour).

Mitted
White feet.

Modified wedge
A type of head that is triangular shaped and not as extreme as a wedge.

Moggie
Non-pedigreed cat.

Monorchid
Male cat with one testicle.

Mutation
A genetic change that alters a cat's characteristics.

Natural breeding
Breeding without the interference of selective breeding.

Necklace
Continuous or broken stripes on the upper part of the chest in tabby varieties.

Neuter
To remove a male cat's testicles by castration so it cannot reproduce.

Nictating membrane
Third eyelid that a cat can pull across its eye for additional protection.

Non-agouti
Not a genetic tabby.

Nose leather
The hairless tip of the nose and nostrils.

Nose liner
Coloured line of skin found across the top of the nose leather in silvers and tabbies.

Not for breeding
A cat that has been sold or registered without breeding rights.

OE
Odd-eyed. Each eye is a different colour.

Outcross
Breeding two cats that have no common ancestors for at least three generations.

Overshot jaw
When the upper jaw protrudes abnormally beyond the lower jaw.

Parasite
Organism that lives off of another one, drinking blood or living in the digestive tract.

Patched tabby
Cats that are any of the tabby patterns (classic, mackerel, ticked or spotted) with patches of red colouring.

Parti-colour
A colour division for cats at cat shows that usually includes bicolours, tortoiseshells and tortie and whites. In any case, the cat must have a solid block of colour with additional colours although the specific definition varies between cat associations.

Pedigree
A document containing names, titles, colours and registration numbers of cat's ancestors.

Pedigreed
To describe a cat that has a pedigree document. Often used interchangeably but incorrectly with 'purebred'.

Phenotype
Visible characteristics of a cat's genetic make-up.

Piebald
Basic white pattern with areas of colour.

Pigment
Colouration.

Pinking up
Describes how a cat's nipples turn bright pink when they have been bred, which happens about three weeks after mating.

Platinum
A silvery-beige colour.

Points/pointed
Coat pattern in cats with a paler body colour, with contrasting darker colours on the face, ears, tail and legs.

Progeny
Offspring of an individual cat.

Provisional
Class at cat shows for cat breeds that have not yet been accepted for championship status by a particular cat association.

Purebred
A cat whose parents are the same or allowable outcrosses.

Quarantine
Time in which a cat is isolated from other cats in order to prevent the possible spread of a disease.

Queen
Female cat used for breeding purposes.

Quick
Vein that runs through a cat's claw.

Rangy
Long body.

Recessive
Gene not expressed unless both members of a specific gene pair are recessive.

Red
Solid cat colour.

Red lynx point
Points that are reddish orange with underlying tabby patterns.

Registry
Cat associations register cats, issue registration numbers, determine breed standards, license cat shows and license cat-show judges.

Reverse tortie/reverse blue-cream
When colour is dominantly red or cream. Also called 'hot tortie/hot blue-cream'.

Rex
Type of coat with no guard hairs but a soft and curly undercoat.

Ringworm
Contagious skin disease caused by a fungus.

Roll out doming
Nicely rounded forehead.

Roman nose
Nose type with an arch and low-set nostrils.

Ruddy
Dark ginger-red colour.

Ruff
A mass of long hair circling the neck, especially on a Persian. Also called 'frill'.

Sable
Dark brown cat colour.

SC
Subcutaneous – under the skin. Also 'SQ'.

Sclera
White portion of the eyeball.

Seal lynx point
Dark, nearly black points with underlying tabby pattern.

Seal point
Dark points, nearly black.

Seal tortie lynx point
Dark points, nearly black with tortoiseshell colouring and an underlying tabby pattern.

Seal tortie point
Primarily dark points, nearly black with an underlying tortoiseshell colour pattern.

Selective breeding
Intentional mating of two cats in order to achieve a trait or to eliminate a trait.

Self
Cat that is of one solid colour from the base to the tip of the hair shaft.

Semi-cobby
Having a slightly longer and leaner body type than cobby.

Semi-foreign
Cat body type that is long and tubular but not as extreme as a cat with a foreign or oriental body type.

Set type
Breeding term to describe the process of breeding successive generations of cats with certain characteristics in the hope of producing cats that will possess the trait and also be able to pass it along to their offspring.

Sex-linked
A characteristic that is usually associated with only one of the sexes.

Shaded
Cat that is white at the base with the darker colour starting halfway down the hair shaft and extending to the tip.

Silver
Cat colour usually the result of a white coat with black ticking.

Single coat
One coat, usually the topcoat or guard hairs, without the downy undercoat.

Sire
Male parent of a kitten.

Slinky
Slang term for a cat breed that is long and slender like a Siamese or Oriental.

Smoke
Cat colour that is white at the base and with darker colouring covering most of the hair shaft.

Solid
One-colour cat.

Spay
Female cat that has been sterilized through a surgical procedure. To alter a female cat so she can no longer breed.

Spectacles
The lighter coloured hair area encircling the eyes. Also called 'goggles'.

Spontaneous mutation
Genetic accident that permanently alters certain genetic characteristics.

Spotted
Coat pattern featuring clear, non-overlapping oval or round spots.

Spotting
White areas in the coat.

SQ
Subcutaneous – under the skin. Also 'SC'.

Standard
The written description of the ideal characteristics of a recognized cat breed.

Stop
Well-pronounced angle between nose and forehead. Indentation on the bridge of the nose, usually between the eyes. Also called 'break'.

Stud
Breeding male cat.

Stumpy
Manx with a tail 1–10 cm ($3/8$–4 in) long, consisting of one to three caudal vertebrae.

Taurine
An amino acid that a cat has to get in a diet for good eyesight.

TICA
The International Cat Association.

Ticking/ticked
Alternating bands of light and dark colour on each individual hair such as found on the Abyssinian.

Tipped/tipping
Colour on the ends of hair.

Toe tufts
Long hairs growing from between the toes, both on the top and underside of the paw.

Tom cat
Unaltered male cat.

Tuck up
Underbelly of a cat, curving up into the haunches.

Tufts
Hair on the tips of the ears and or between the cat's toes.

Umbilical hernia
Hernia of fat and sometimes the intestines in the region of the naval.

Undercoat
Soft and downy hairs next to the skin.

Undershot jaw
When the lower jaw protrudes abnormally beyond the upper jaw.

Van
A colour pattern on a bicolour or calico with colour confined to head and tail with only one or two small body spots.

Variety
A subgroup of a breed. A cat that has registered parents but is not eligible for championship status because it does not conform to the breed standard.

Vascular
Pertaining to the blood vessels.

Weaning
When kittens learn to eat solid food and no longer rely on their mother to feed them.

Wedge
Head type that has triangular-shaped dimensions.

Weegie
Slang term for Norwegian Forest Cat.

Whip tail
Long, thin, flexible tail tapering from the base to the tip, typical of a Siamese.

Whisker pad
Area of the upper lip from which the whiskers grow. The fleshy part of the muscle on either side of the muzzle below the nose.

Whisker pinch
The distinct demarcation between the cheeks and the muzzle.

White
Cat colour that lacks pigmentation.

Whole
A cat that is capable of reproduction has not been spayed or neutered.

Wry bite
Crooked jaw.

Woolly
Thick undercoat.

Zoonosis
An animal disease that can be spread to humans.

Index